The Oxford Anthology of
African-American Poetry

THE OXFORD ANTHOLOGY

of

AFRICAN-AMERICAN POETRY

Edited by
ARNOLD RAMPERSAD

Associate Editor
HILARY HERBOLD

OXFORD
UNIVERSITY PRESS
2006

OXFORD
UNIVERSITY PRESS

Oxford University Press, Inc., publishes works that further
Oxford University's objective of excellence
in research, scholarship, and education.

Oxford   New York
Auckland   Cape Town   Dar es Salaam   Hong Kong   Karachi
Kuala Lumpur   Madrid   Melbourne   Mexico City   Nairobi
New Delhi   Shanghai   Taipei   Toronto

With offices in
Argentina   Austria   Brazil   Chile   Czech Republic   France   Greece
Guatemala   Hungary   Italy   Japan   Poland   Portugal   Singapore
South Korea   Switzerland   Thailand   Turkey   Ukraine   Vietnam

Copyright © 2006 by Oxford University Press, Inc.

Published by Oxford University Press, Inc.
198 Madison Avenue, New York, New York 10016
www.oup.com

Oxford is a registered trademark of Oxford University Press

Library of Congress Cataloging-in-Publication Data
The Oxford anthology of African-American poetry.
p.   cm.
ISBN-13: 978-0-19-512563-4
ISBN-10: 0-19-512563-0
1. American poetry—African American authors.   2. African American—Poetry.
PS591.N4097 2005
811.008'0896073—dc22   2005015242

3   5   7   9   8   6   4
Printed in the United States of America
on acid-free paper

for

Nellie Y. McKay

ACKNOWLEDGMENTS

Compiling this anthology would have been much more arduous without the assistance of various individuals. Dr. Hilary Herbold at Princeton University was my first associate on the project. I remain grateful to her for her energy and dedication in helping me gather and sift a vast amount of poetry in order to lay its foundation. Later on, Dr. Meta DuEwa Jones, at Stanford University, assisted in many ways. Her love of the subject and her skill in organizing the material proved to be invaluable. I thank Luke Marshall Rickford, who worked hard on the anthology over a summer away from his undergraduate studies. Todd Dapremont of Stanford University helped later, with diligence and sound judgment, as the project moved to its conclusion.

I also owe an incalculable debt to the veteran poet Everett Hoagland, who for many years was a professor of English at the University of Massachusetts at Dartmouth. His deep knowledge of the subject of African-American poetry led me time and again to poets whose writings I have included here. I thank him for his timely intervention in the project, as well as for his generosity and his various suggestions for improving the book.

Other poets and scholars, too numerous for me to name here, helped me to find poets or eased the way for me to publish poems. I refer, for example, to Elizabeth Alexander, Mari Evans, Nathaniel Mackey, Harryette Mullen, Xavier Nicholas, Sianne Ngai, David Wallace, Eugene Redmond, Lamont B. Steptoe, and Richard Yarborough.

I must also acknowledge the help at Oxford University Press of various editors and assistants, who have been patient over the years since T. Susan Chang, then the Humanities editor, commissioned the book. Her successor, Elissa Morris, has supported it shrewdly from start to finish. Also at Oxford, I owe much to Jeremy Lewis and Eve Bachrach.

In thanking these individuals, I know that I have missed mentioning others who deserve to be mentioned. For such lapses I apologize, but my gratitude remains sincere for all who helped to make this book possible.

Arnold Rampersad
Stanford University

CONTENTS

Contents

Contents

5. IF WE MUST DIE

8. Is She Our Sister?

9. Don't It Make You Want to Cry?

10. WHOSE CHILDREN ARE THESE?

11. THEY ARE ALL OF ME

Contents

12. OH, SINGING TREE!

13. OH, MY SOUL IS IN THE WHIRLWIND!

14. DEAR LOVELY DEATH

15. I DREAM A WORLD

INTRODUCTION

When the editors at Oxford University Press asked me some years ago to put together an anthology of poems by black Americans, they were firm about one point. This collection was not to be a historical survey of verse by black Americans, much less a "scholarly" edition replete with footnotes, but rather one designed to paint a portrait of African-American life and culture achieved through the medium of poetry written by African-Americans themselves. In turn, my associate editor and I had one idea about which we were also firm. We would not include a poem simply because it was thought to be of historical importance, or of some other significance, if we saw it as also technically flawed in some obvious way. One result of this decision is that many familiar poems will not be found in this collection.

Instead, we set out to compile an anthology that would form, as accurately and imaginatively as we could do so, a composite picture in poetry of black American culture. Toward that end, we divided our anthology into sections aimed at illuminating different, defining aspects of African-American life and culture. For example, the first section is devoted to the art and practice of writing poetry. While writing fine verse is a challenge for everyone committed to the art, being black in America often complicates and even threatens the role of the poet and the practice of poetry. Exceptions exist, but the black American poet, especially in the last two generations, typically endures an uneasy relationship to the canon of European and American poetry. This estrangement exists, obviously, because of the extent to which the depressed position of blacks within the nation has served to alienate them from the standards and values of the dominant culture. That lowly position is the result of centuries of slavery, segregation, and other denials of human rights to the black American world. Even today, when laws exist to protect the civil rights of blacks, a tragic discrepancy often exists between these legal freedoms, on the one hand, and the reality of racism, on the other.

This history has tended to alienate the black poet and lover of verse from the tradition of poetry written by whites. Such poetry usually has been written out of social and cultural assumptions that black poets, and black people, had not been allowed to share in the past and are inconsistently allowed to share in the present. This alienation often extends to the English language itself, as the principal medium for expressing those assumptions. To love the English language is a challenge to many black poets, but all poets ideally should love their native language if they are to do justice to their emotions, ideas, and ambitions as literary artists.

Having laid the groundwork for our anthology in this first section, we proceed to offer other sections of poetry that also speak to major aspects of African-American culture. In sections on Africa, slavery, and the South, we represent the poets as they meditate on history. One section looks into that vivid center of complication within black culture: the shifting, controversial place, over the centuries, of Africa in the hearts and minds of black Americans. Africa was, and to some black people still is, the ancestral repository of hope and pride. It also was, and to some people still is, a primary source of doubt, ignorance, confusion, and shame. Aided by historians, but also by the will to believe differently, many black Americans have been able to refute the idea of Africa as the "Dark Continent," the land of pagan gloom in comparison to the Judeo-Christian centers of European and Euro-American civilization. Still the sense of negativity and notoriety persists. It derives most notably from the almost entirely derogatory depiction of Africa, until recently, in movies, books, and magazines; it also has something to do, surely, with brooding on the idea that Africans were complicit in the slave trade. For generations, whites depicted Africa as a land of barbarism. Over the centuries, the black poet has both absorbed many of these harsh judgments and also resisted them. Some poets have done both, with the struggle between these opposed perceptions helping to create poetry that reflects the intrinsic complexity of African-American culture.

Similarly, the black poet has responded to the depressing presence of slavery itself as a feature—perhaps the defining feature—of black American identity. Although slavery was abolished, its impact lives on. Even today, many people, especially those who live in the South, see around them tokens and mementos of slavery. They see evocations of slavery in the public flaunting of the Confederate flag, even if those who fly the flag do not mean to defend slavery. To many African-Americans slavery is a fact of history that must be suppressed and forgotten, lest it corrode the black mind and spirit. (Booker T. Washington and other blacks, especially proselytizers for Christianity, even represented slavery as an essentially beneficent institution.) To other African-Americans, equally forward looking, slavery must be recalled and pondered for that same basic reason: to blunt its destructive power. Black poets have been sensitive to this tension. Their poetry typically reflects perhaps the most crucial question posed by historians about slavery in America. Did it destroy virtually all vestiges of African culture in the American slave—and, with this destruction, the humanity of the black man and woman? Or did sustaining elements of the African past survive the mental erasures of slavery, and in so doing helped to ensure the nurturing of black humanity?

This anthology looks separately, but in a related manner, at the South. Seen first as the prime killing ground of slavery, then of Jim Crow and lynch law, the South has paradoxically also shone as the best of all possible settings for the growth of African-American culture. Once the main site of racial humiliation, the region has also been seen by many black Americans as a beloved ground. For many black nationalists, only Africa can truly be home. For many more people, however, the South is home. The migration of millions of blacks to the North did not sever the ties between those fleeing the South and those who stayed behind. If the idea of the North found its center in new freedoms, that idea quickly faced the reality of urban decay and feelings of dislocation, isolation, and even alienation. The flaws of the South were well known but so were its charms. The South bespeaks for many blacks not simply the pleasures of fertile fields, lazy streams, and cool, inviting woods but also the treasure of kinship and community lost or at risk in the North. Now, according to demographers, blacks are returning to the South in great numbers—a movement that the black poet prophesied in the many works that deal realistically with both its appeal and its violent history.

Aiming for even greater intimacy, this anthology features, in separate sections, poetry that addresses the interrelated subjects of the black man, the black woman, and the black child.

The black man has been a singularly compelling figure in the American imagination. First as a slave to be broken and exploited as chattel, stripped of dignity or authority, the black man has borne, and continues to bear, a burden of uncommon weight in American culture. Associated with fears of his alleged sexual excessiveness, his capacity for criminality, and virtually any other flaw of character that would facilitate his suppression, the black man may be, second only to protest against injustice, the central subject of African-American poetry. If the "Negro," as Richard Wright put it, is America's metaphor, then the "Negro" man is the epitome of that metaphor. Both male and female poets have explored the nuances of the idea of black manhood in America. They have done so at times critically, with searing candor, but also with compassion and a will to understand the unique pressures visited upon black men in a society that has yet to come to terms with its fear of them.

The black woman constitutes a subject both related to and quite distinct from that of the black man. Here, too, we are concerned with poetic treatments by both women and men. Demurely and even timidly in the earliest generations, poetry by and about the black woman has grown in technical range and insight. In her own, different way, as compared to the experience of the black man, the black woman has had to face damning assumptions and imputations that have also questioned her humanity. Debasing ideas about her sexuality and psychology, encouraged (as with the black man) for the purpose of making her a more pliable servant, have clouded her image. Prevailing criteria of feminine beauty have worked to demoralize her. In our own time, with the evolving condition of the African-American family, the black woman has seen her burden grow. The black poet has responded to this ongoing crisis of representation with skill and vigor. Spurred on by the renaissance of American literary feminism and of American feminism in general, black female poets, like black women novelists of the same era, have taken possession of the subject of the black woman, rather than address it according to some alienated position.

The black child, too, has also served as a vital inspiration to the poet. Over the generations, the child has been perhaps the most poignant symbol both of despair and hope, of cynicism and optimism. Here, too, might be seen an example of the ways in which African-American poetry must be different from its mainstream counterpart. In canonical poetry written in English, except in the works of poets such as Wordsworth and Blake, the child possesses little significance as a subject. Indeed, poetry about the child leads all too easily to sentimentality, a tendency that also attends the poetry that blacks write about their children. However, the social and historical reality surrounding the black child typically makes that child a more compelling, freighted subject. The black poet has recognized the special, indispensable aspect of this subject. If sentimentality is the bane of poetry written about children, the black poet nevertheless must be prepared to risk even banality to arrive at truths that are peculiar to his or her culture. The black poet has done so.

The most durable thread binding this trinity—man, woman, and child—has been the ideals of family and love, which inspire special sections in this anthology. Love here must be defined in its full scope—familial, romantic, sexual, and spiritual. The black poet has aimed to engage these multiple levels of meaning. In the worst days of slavery and of scientific racism, blacks were often said to be incapable of genuine love; they were said to lack that refinement of spirit on which the "highest" forms of love build. This denial had sinister benefits for those who wished, again, to push blacks to the margin of civilization, the easier to exploit them. Just as Thomas Jefferson questioned the capacity of blacks to love, many of the practices and laws underwriting slavery depended to some extent on the denial of the possibility of genuine love among blacks. Thus husband and wife (if marriage were permitted) could be separated, sold, and dispatched in opposite directions. So too, with children, who could be sold away from mother and father with impunity. The idea of the emotional shallowness of blacks was, and is, a crucial fiction of white racism. A primary task of serious black poets has been to reclaim and rehabilitate the notion of the vitality of love in their world.

Religion deserves its own section because of its virtual supremacy among black social institutions. Whether in the animism of slaves fresh from Africa, or in the rituals of Catholicism, Protestantism, Islam, and other faiths, religion has sustained the black world. It has meant the rod of Puritan discipline, the straight and narrow path to salvation; it has also meant fatalistic release from the trials and traumas of the world; it has often meant paradox, which some African-Americans have attempted to resolve by worshipping the idea of a Black Christ. Some poets have seen the laws of Christianity as essentially opposed to the rhythms of the black body, which longs for the supposed freedom of pagan Africa. The music and drama of the black church, its ecstatic cries and elaborate sermons, have entranced many writers otherwise immune to the spell of religion. To some blacks, also, Christianity has made blacks into a docile people, unwilling to fight their enemies—although many of the leaders of the civil rights movement, such as Martin Luther King, Jr., were ministers. To believers, religion has meant solace and wisdom, the one reliable resource in the struggle for inner peace. The black poet has spoken to the importance and the paradoxes of this aspect of the culture.

Rivaling and in some ways surpassing religion as a therapy, music has also shaped the work of black poets. In the days of slavery, out of the blending of African musicality and Christian belief, came the famed "Negro" spirituals. In words but also in rhythms and harmonies, in plaintive melodies and assertive tones, the spirituals epitomized the sanctity of African-American belief and also, at their best, the possession of artistic genius. However, if the spiritual was the auspicious beginning of black America's musical reputation, it was certainly not the end. Ragtime, blues, jazz, bebop, gospel, rhythm and blues, rock, rap—music, religious or secular, from the serene to the frenetic, has been the most irresistible mode of African-American cultural expression.

Although seldom seen as such, the genius of the black musician has been both boon and menace to the black poet. The vitality of that music, its ability to adapt and change, to originate and create, and to prophesize social change, have formed a constant challenge to the poet. Certainly this challenge has been felt by poets since the 1920s. In the Harlem Renaissance, the language of the blues was first identified by gifted writers—notably Zora Neale Hurston and Langston Hughes—as speaking cultural truth in ways that often put the typical black poet to shame. This dominance of music and its strong influence over the nation has led to something like a permanent, if still largely unacknowledged, crisis of vocation among black poets. In comparison to the fame of many black musicians, the poet exists, with few exceptions, in oblivion. How the black writer has coped with life in the shadow of black music is a story in itself. Suffice it to say that the black poet has explored the allure and also the challenge posed by the black musician and his or her rival art.

In black America, who leads? This anthology, which reserves one section for poetry as a vehicle of protest against social injustice in America, reserves another for tributary poetry, or verse by black poets which recognizes the black hero. By black heroism we mean, in particular, the actions of men and women who have dared to lead their fellow blacks toward freedom and power. From the poet Phillis Wheatley and the slave rebel Nat Turner to the abolitionists Frederick Douglass and Sojourner Truth, from W.E.B. Du Bois to Rosa Parks and Martin Luther King, Jr., blacks have been willing to pay the price of standing up against injustice. Black poets have recognized the need to remember the deeds of such people. In the emptiness where tributes in marble and stone should stand, black poets offer their crafted words so that future generations might remember such men and woman and their sacrifices.

Religion-haunted in many ways, blacks historically have seen death as a phenomenon neither to fear nor to revile but to accept as a natural part of the fabric of their culture. Death, accordingly, is a major—but not always solemn—theme in black poetry. It provides the occasion for expressing both sorrow and satire, muted grieving and eloquence. The concept of death as deliverance from slavery (sometimes with flights of the soul back to Africa), or as release from the trauma or even the shabbiness of everyday life, has inspired many black poets. So, too, with death in its more specific forms—the death of father and mother, as in compositions by Claude McKay or Gwendolyn Brooks; or the death of children, as in the work of Michael S. Harper. Death as the occasion for transcendence, essential to the Western elegiac tradition, also has its counterpart in African-American verse.

To conclude this anthology and its attempt at a composite portrait of black America, we have assembled a selection of poems in which the black poet, eschewing calls to social or political, looks instead toward ideal imaginings of the future. Once, African-American poets sang optimistically about the future almost always in religious lyrics about life beyond death. Nevertheless, black poets have also dreamt of a world in which humanity finds it possible to move at last beyond prejudice and bigotry, beyond the old, bloody divisions of color, race, creed, and culture. Some black poets have imagined, as part of their vocation, a healed, whole world built on idealistic notions of justice, trust, and love. Sometimes inspired by religion, as in the case of Robert Hayden, or out of a more secular hope, as with Langston Hughes, these poets have taken on the blessed burden of humane prophecy. They have imagined something like heaven on earth, implausible perhaps but precious to the psychological and spiritual wellbeing of their people.

Doubtless there are aspects of the black experience, unrepresented in this anthology, that might be isolated fruitfully with selections from the library of black poets. Nevertheless, we hope that we have come close to succeeding in our goal of allowing a cross-section of these poets to create with their own words a portrait of their people.

Although a composite portrait is our choice here, African-American poetry has had an orderly history. Changing and growing, it was created on the whole not by naïve men and women but by artists who knew something of the tradition of poetry in English. Their poetry did not sprout wildly or spontaneously but rather evolved slowly, painstakingly. Its history begins in the eighteenth century, with the work of Phillis Wheatley, who arrived at Boston as a slave from Africa when only seven or eight years of age. Encouraged by a kindly master, Wheatley saw her book *Poems on Various Subjects, Religious and Moral*, published in London in 1773 as only the second book of verse ever published by an American woman—and the first by any black American. A devout Christian, she engaged both conventional themes and others related to her life as a black. She wrote decorously, according to the practices of her day, about subjects such as reason and imagination; she wrote several elegies. A poem celebrates the heroic grandeur of George Washington, who received her as a visitor to his camp one day during the Revolutionary War. However, her work also touches on Africa and slavery, on the efforts of blacks in art and religion, and on the paradox of the black American poet.

With his volume of verse *The Hope of Liberty* (1829), George Moses Horton, a slave poet, became the first black American to use verse to protest against slavery. Thereafter, protest and black poetry would be a common union, although black poets also sought a broader definition of their role. Frances Ellen Watkins Harper, perhaps the most representative of black writers of the nineteenth century, protested against slavery in volumes such as her antebellum *Poems on Miscellaneous Subjects*, but she was also a pioneer in writing about black women. Other skilled and representative writers arose after the Civil War. James D. Corrothers, in offering verse in both dialect and standard English, helped to establish one of the persisting tensions in black poetry. Dialect verse, based on stereotypes of black character arising mainly from an idealized vision of slavery, was the most popular development in black American poetry in the later nineteenth century. Its true genius would be Paul Laurence Dunbar of Ohio, who became the first black American poet to achieve a national reputation, with volumes such as *Oak and Ivy* (1893) and *Lyrics of Lowly Life* (1896). His brilliant execution of verse about music and dance, humor and vernacular culture, heroism and spirituality, in both dialect and standard English, makes him one of the major figures in African-American verse.

In the first two decades of the twentieth century, other representative poets emerged. James Weldon Johnson, William Stanley Braithwaite, and Fenton Johnson offered three different versions of the modern black poet. James Weldon Johnson bridged the old and new, in that he wrote both dialect and standard verse; he was also the first true anthologist of black verse. His *God's Trombones* (1927) is a classic of the Harlem Renaissance, but his two editions of his anthology *The Book of American Negro Poetry* (1922 and 1931) are crucial both for their verse and his astute introductions. In contrast, William Stanley Braithwaite of Boston ignored race, as some black poets have always done, in favor of a "universal" vision of the poet. Finally, Fenton Johnson of Chicago was the most dedicated modernist of the three. In the landmark *Poetry* magazine founded by Harriet Munroe, and elsewhere, he published poetry stripped of hoary poeticisms, disdainful of dialect, and reflective of the new realities of life in a new century.

These poets set the stage for the first outpouring of black American literature—the Harlem Renaissance of the 1920s. While this movement was dominated by music (jazz and blues, with performers such as Bessie Smith, Louis Armstrong, and Duke Ellington), and included fiction, drama, painting, sculpture, and other arts, poetry was also prominent. Two young men stood out as rival versions of the black poet. Countee Cullen, who loved traditional, mainly British writers (especially Keats and A.E. Houseman), wrote movingly about racism, the conflict he felt between his black body and his strict Christian faith, and the paradox of being black and a poet. He marveled that God could do "this curious thing: / To make a poet black and bid him sing!" Langston Hughes, however, urged young blacks to embrace black culture and resist middle-class restraints. His poetry expressed his love of ordinary black people, his hatred of social injustice, and his near-reverence for the blues. Starting with *The Weary Blues* (1926), he published verse into the 1960s, by which time he was widely known as the poet laureate of black America.

Other poets of the Harlem Renaissance expanded the range of black poetry. The Jamaican-born Claude McKay began with dialect verse but later excelled also as a lyric poet writing in Standard English who also used his art to protest vehemently against injustice. Georgia Douglas Johnson wrote mainly of genteel women and genteel love. Arna Bontemps' strong Seventh Day Adventist background led him to create meditative verse. Anne Spencer was perhaps the most avowedly modernist poet of the movement, with her emphasis on privacy of vision, complexity of allusions, and syntactical denseness.

The Depression saw little poetry, except for the work of Hughes and Sterling Brown, a Howard University professor who also valued blues culture and its strong black men and women. Now Hughes emphasized poems about radical socialism, in which he indicted imperialism and capitalism. In the 1940s, however, poetry flowered again. Margaret Walker won the annual Yale University Younger Poets prize for her slender volume *For My People* (1942). The title poem is a mixture of Whitman and Hughes, a rhythmic tribute to the black masses and their culture, as well as an exhortation to them to rise up and assert their freedom. Robert Hayden of Detroit first wrote verse that showed his extensive reading in black history. Later, especially in poems about the slave trade but also in pieces about domestic life, he emerged as a technical master, moderately modernist in style. His work, while still embracing black interests, also acknowledged the values of his Bah'ai faith, which emphasizes the unity of people everywhere. Melvin B. Tolson of Oklahoma, entranced by the dense, highly allusive, poetry of Ezra Pound, now emerged as the black poet most clearly dedicated to radical modernist values, as in his *Libretto for the Republic of Liberia*. Gwendolyn Brooks, also a modernist but determined to write about the urban black experience from a woman's point of view, produced an admirable body of work. In 1950, African-American poetry reached a milestone when she became the first black writer to win the Pulitzer Prize for Poetry—for *Annie Allen* (1949).

With the civil rights turmoil of the later 1950s and the rise of the separatist Black Arts movement of the 1960s and early 1970s, black poetry underwent a revolution. Hundreds of thousands of volumes of poetry (many were pamphlets) were sold, as blacks radically reexamined their place in American society. The most talented poet was probably LeRoi Jones of Newark, New Jersey. First a young poet-editor in the mainly white "Beat" movement centered in Greenwich Village in Manhattan (as in his touching 1961 book of poems *Preface to a Twenty-Volume Suicide Note*), in 1965 Jones left the Village for Harlem. As the leader of the Black Arts movement, he repudiated white culture. Changing his name to Amiri Baraka, he wrote poetry of such vituperation and sardonic wit that he influenced a generation of writers. Poets of separate sensibilities, styles, and degrees of skill, unified by their surging new racial consciousness, emerged. These included Don L. Lee, later Haki Madhubuti (his slender volume of 1969, *Don't Cry, Scream* was a bestseller), Sonia Sanchez, Etheridge Knight, Mari Evans, Nikki Giovanni, Carolyn Rodgers, and Audre Lorde. Most of the new writers had in common a distrust of white people and white culture, a fondness for vernacular speech and culture, a reverence for black music, a readiness to match poetic form to the volatility of the age, and a desire to reach a wide black audience. Publishers, notably Dudley Randall's Broadside Press, brought out race-inspired books and pamphlets of verse that few mainstream, white publishers would have touched.

Many of the poets who flourished in the 1960s and early 1970s publish much less after the civil rights and Black Power movements passed into history. Volumes of poetry ceased to appear in great quantity. In many ways, the age became more prosaic, and more materialistic. Some poets of the earlier era continued to write, but often with altered sensibilities that reflected the arrival of a more sober, perhaps more chastened sense of American political reality. Excellent younger writers emerged. Michael S. Harper, in volumes such as *Nightmare Begins Responsibility* (1975), fused the passion and rebellious creativity of an earlier time with a broadening vision of the human experience and a more cosmopolitan sense of the literary tradition. However, although fine poetry continued to be written by a number of black poets, the main literary phenomenon was probably the emergence, as the feminist movement gathered power, of novelists such as Alice Walker, Gloria Naylor, Toni Cade Bambara, Gayle Jones, and, above all, Toni Morrison, who would win the Nobel Prize for Literature.

Despite the popularity of black novelists, as the new century began black American poetry had perhaps a broader base than ever before, and a more settled sense of achievement. Writers, some veteran, others relatively young, and covering a wide range of poetic practice, published with confidence and skill. The most honored new voice was probably that of Rita Dove, who not only won the Pulitzer Prize for poetry but also served as Poet Laureate of the United States from 1993 to 1995. Nathaniel Mackey and Harryette Mullen, in separate ways, covered the spectrum from the esotericism and difficulties of "language" poetry to the simpler, blues-driven eloquence accessible to ordinary readers. Lucille Clifton, a veteran poet, was honored repeatedly for books such as *Quilting: Poems 1987–1990*. June Jordan, a radical feminist and leftist political critic, brought these concerns brilliantly into the public sphere through her verse. Maya Angelou, better known as an autobiographer, added to her prestige—and that of the black poet—when she read a poem, as Robert Frost had done at President Kennedy's inauguration in 1960, at President Clinton's inauguration in 1992.

Such honors and awards suggest the arrival of African-American poetry on the national scene—a far cry from the first scribbling of the lonely

African slave girl in Boston, Phillis Wheatley, who mastered English as a foreign tongue, and who made herself into a poet to begin the humane and artistic tradition that this anthology seeks to honor.

Arnold Rampersad
Stanford University

The Oxford Anthology of
African-American Poetry

1.

TO MAKE A POET BLACK

Today's News

ELIZABETH ALEXANDER

Heavyweight champion of the world Mike Tyson
broke his fist in a street brawl in Harlem
at three A.M. outside an all-night clothing store
where he was buying an 800-dollar, white
leather coat. The other dude, on TV, said,
"It was a sucker punch." Muhammad Ali said
Tyson ain't pretty enough to be heavyweight
champion of the world. Years ago a new Ali
threw his Olympic gold into the Ohio
River, said he'd get it when black people were truly
free in this country. In South Africa there is a dance
that says   we are fed up   we have no work   you have
struck a rock. I saw it on today's news.

I didn't want to write a poem that said "blackness
is," because we know better than anyone
that we are not one or ten or ten thousand things
Not one poem   We could count ourselves forever
and never agree on the number. When the first
black Olympic gymnast was black and on TV I called
home to say it was colored on channel three
in nineteen eighty-eight. Most mornings these days
Ralph Edwards comes into the bedroom and says, "Elizabeth,
this is your life. Get up and look for color,
look for color everywhere."

when i stand around among poets

LUCILLE CLIFTON

1

when i stand around among poets
i am embarrassed mostly,
their long white heads,
the great bulge in their pants,

their certainties

i don't know how to do
what i do in the way
that i do it. it happens
despite me and i pretend

to deserve it.

but i don't know how to do it.
only sometimes when
something is singing
i listen and so far

i hear.

2

when i stand around
among poets, sometimes
i hear a single music
in us, one note
dancing us through the
singular moving world.

Flame

Jayne Cortez

And it's familiar
this fact of flame
of indulging images
the salty dust devil winds
spitting into silver helmets
through shit splattered wings
the beginnings and endings
in which i salute the sun
because i know it has to come today
because a dream is like a nail
because this room peels back the hole in my cup
and so i tell you whoever you are
plastic pen, paper, dictionary
i tell you
the policemen sing
the sanitation men whistle
the distended body of military parades
fly flags in wounds of dead words
and the sad look of tribal warfare
points every second between sockets
into the same flame of the zero hour
and i know it has to come from me

Nexus

Rita Dove

I wrote stubbornly into the evening.
At the window, a giant praying mantis
rubbed his monkey wrench head against the glass,
begging vacantly with pale eyes;

and the commas leapt at me like worms
or miniature scythes blackened with age.
The praying mantis screeched louder,
his ragged jaws opening onto formlessness.

I walked outside;
the grass hissed at my heels.
Up ahead in the lapping darkness
he wobbled, magnified and absurdly green,
a brontosaurus, a poet.

To the Pale Poets

Ray Durem

I know I'm not sufficiently obscure
to please the critics—nor devious enough.
Imagery escapes me.
I cannot find those mild and gracious words
to clothe the carnage.
Blood is blood and murder's murder.
What's a lavender word for lynch?
Come, you pale poets, wan, refined and dreamy:
here is a black woman working out her guts
in a white man's kitchen
for little money and no glory.
How should I tell that story?
There is a black boy, blacker still from death,
face down in the cold Korean mud.
Come on with your effervescent jive
explain to him why he ain't alive.
Reword our specific discontent
into some plaintive melody,
a little whine, a little whimper,
not too much—and no rebellion!
God, no! Rebellion's much too corny.
You deal with finer feelings,
very subtle—an autumn leaf
hanging from a tree—I see a body!

Why Do So Few Blacks Study Creative Writing?

CORNELIUS EADY

Always the same, sweet hurt,
The understanding that settles in the eyes
Sooner or later, at the end of class,
In the silence cooling in the room.
Sooner or later it comes to this,

You stand face to face with your
Younger face and you have to answer
A student, a young woman this time,

And you're alone in the classroom
Or in your office, a day or so later,
And she has to know, if all music
Begins equal, why this poem of hers
Needed a passport, a glossary,

A disclaimer. *It was as if I were* . . .
What? Talking for the first time?
Giving yourself up? Away?
There are worlds, and there are worlds,
She reminds you. She needs to know
What's wrong with me? and you want

To crowbar or spade her hurt
To the air. You want photosynthesis
To break it down to an organic language.
You want to shake *I hear you*
Into her ear, armor her life

With permission. Really, what
Can I say? That if she chooses
To remain here the term
Neighborhood will always have
A foreign stress, that there
Will always be the moment

The small, hard details
Of your life will be made
To circle their wagons?

Puttin' On The Dog

for "Corner Girl"

EVERETT HOAGLAND

Is my shit correct?
Is my vine correct?
Are my kicks country or correct??
Is my "do" down?

Is my shit correct?

Is my rusty black dic-
tion correct?
Should my ever more erudite
utterances be in "The Vernacular?"
Should my presentation be
theatrical and spectacular?

Is my shit correct?

Should my manner be mannered
and laid back??
Is my poetry *Poesy*?
Does it go too far into *haute couture
noire*?
Does it come from hard facts
and Fanon,
or does it refer repeatedly
to *The Canon* trippin'
in *Trickster Mode*, tryin'
to *Trope*-A-Dope?????

Is my shit correct?

But, hey, black poetry's got more
than one good way.

The other day I asked a young Blood
poet if my stuff was correct, if it was
happenin'.
He said, Breaklight becomes dawn,
Ol' Head. The *word* "happenin"
ain't happenin', ain't "where it's at."
Today it's *on*. Word!
Our work is *all that*.

"Michaelangelo" the Elder

BOB KAUFMAN

I live alone, like pith in a tree,
My teeth rattle, like musical instruments.
In one ear a spider spins its web of eyes,
In the other a cricket chirps all night,
This is the end,
Which art, that proves my glory has brought me.
I would die for Poetry.

For Black Poets Who Think of Suicide

ETHERIDGE KNIGHT

Black Poets should live—not leap
From steel bridges (Like the white boys do.
Black Poets should *live*—not lay
Their necks on railroad tracks (like the white boys do.
Black Poets should seek—but not search too much
In sweet dark caves, nor hunt for snipe
Down psychic trails (like the white boys do.

For Black Poets belong to Black People. Are
The Flutes of Black Lovers. Are
The Organs of Black Sorrows. Are
The Trumpets of Black Warriors.
Let All Black poets die as trumpets,
And be buried in the dust of marching feet.

Bloodbirth

Audre Lorde

That which is inside of me screaming
beating about for exit or entry
names the wind, wanting winds' voice
wanting winds' power
it is not my heart
and I am trying to tell this
without art or embellishment
with bits of me flying out in all directions
screams memories old pieces of flesh
struck off like dry bark
from a felled tree, bearing
up or out
holding or bring forth
child or demon
is this birth or exorcism or
the beginning machinery of myself
outlining recalling
my father's business—what I must be
about—my own business
minding.

Shall I split
or be cut down
by a word's complexion or the lack of it
and from what direction
will the opening be made
to show the true face of me
lying exposed and together
my children your children their children
bent on our conjugating business.

Incantation

(for jonetta)

E. ETHELBERT MILLER

let all poems speak and address themselves
let each phrase like hair on a head
comb itself back madame walker style
let the love poems wear gardenias
let the political poems wear suits the way muslims did
during the days of elijah
let the poems be fruitful and multiple

Blah-Blah

HARRYETTE MULLEN

Ack-ack, aye-aye.
Baa baa, Baba, Bambam, Bebe, Berber, Bibi, blah-blah, Bobo,
    bonbon,
booboo, Bora Bora, Boutros Boutros, bye-bye.
Caca, cancan, Cece, cha-cha, chichi, choo-choo, chop chop,
    chow chow, Coco, cocoa,
come come, cuckoo.
Dada, Dee Dee, Didi, dindin, dodo, doodoo, dumdum,
    Duran Duran.
Fifi, fifty-fifty, foofoo, froufrou.
Gaga, Gigi, glug-glug, go-go, goody-goody, googoo, grisgris.
Haha, harhar, hear hear, heehee, hey hey, hip-hip, hoho,
    Hsing-Hsing, hubba-hubba, humhum.
is is, It'sIts.
JarJar, Jo Jo, juju.
Kiki, knock knock, Koko, Kumkum.
Lala, Lili, Ling-Ling looky-looky, Lulu.
Mahi mahi, mama, Mau Mau, Mei-Mei, Mimi, Momo, murmur,
    my my.
Na Na, No-no, now now.
Oh-oh, oink oink.
Pago Pago, Palau Palau, papa, pawpaw, peepee, Phen Fen,
    pooh-pooh, poopoo, pupu, putt-putt.
Rah-rah, ReRe.
Shih-Shih, Sing Sing, Sirhan Sirhan, Sen Sen, Sisi, so-so.
Tata, taki-taki, talky-talky, Tam Tam, Tartar, teetee, Tintin,
    Tingi Tingi, tom-tom, toot toot, tsetse, tsk tsk, tutu,
    tumtum, tut tut.
Van Van, veve, vroom-vroom.
Wahwah, Walla Walla, weewee, win-win.
Yadda yadda Yari Yari, yaya, ylang ylang, yo-yo, yuk-yuk,
    yum-yum.
Zizi, ZsaZsa, Zouzou, Zuzu.

Detroit Addendum—

for Philip Levine

MURRAY JACKSON

Not Virgil, not Beatrice.
You, Philip, took us on slick city streets
to the pimped belch of Detroit

DODGE MAIN WYNADOTTE CHEMICAL FORD ROUGE CHEVROLET GEAR &
      AXLE
in one unbroken line.

Riverrun past burning moat, round
sanguine cauldrons, ending and beginning over again
in a coke-oven shake-out.

From fiery epicenters, black faces,
white faces, glow red. *We stare* through words
into fire until our *eyes are also fire.*

Things passed from hand to hand in darkness
that we, like machines, cannot see.

King Henry's table, seating in split shifts,
neck bones 'n' ribs, corned beef on rye
with mustard, kielbasa and raw onions.

Philip, I do remember a black man,
the Old Boy who danced all night
at Ford Highland Park—my father.

What Work Is is work.

One sees pictures of Dante:

CARL PHILLIPS

in Byzantine profile, looking about
as visionary as the next unremarkable bird;
frozen in an encounter with Beatrice on a
significant bridge or some tumbledown
strada, about to lose her all over again.
My own picture is more plastic:

the maestro, leaning stiffly out
from the roofless carriage of exile,
has his eye on the hands of a particular
young man just off of the roadside, lifting
the salvageable pieces of fruit
from the ground, and in a bucket he has brought
for the purpose, rinsing each separately
free of dirt, then paring away the soft,
inedible portions.
                    It is another of those
afternoons when he can hardly endure
the ride home, he's that eager
to put it all down, that certain that each
of the man's beautiful gestures must
in some way concern the soul.

Poem

(for the Blues Singers)

STERLING PLUMPP

Poems are not places.
There are no maps for centuries
where the geography of skin
is anonymous in memory.
I am a secondhand dream
in concrete slabs of silence.
Somewhere bones speak
for my name / over fibers
of their secrets. My poems
are wanderers, meandering
in crevices between distances
and tombs. Where my voice
is bound with hammering against
the anvil of truth.

Poems are bridges, neon
reaches across worlds
where language seeks
a voice for itself. Where words
are steps up towers
of perception. I exist
in language I invent
out of ruins. Out of
the nameless sand wind
scatters as my soul.
I exist in lines of spirits.
Who gather in longings
blues singers peddle for
sweat. I exist, landless,
cropping my dreams in soil
from distances and silence
only travelers of the Middle Passage
own.

Not About Poems

CAROLYN RODGERS

a lonely poem is nothing
special
    like a lonely person
        you can see them everyday

nobody wants to read a
    lonely poem
like nobody wants to read a
    lonely face
           you see them every day

i can write about love
living high and fine togethers

i can write about mommas, poppas,
show-stoppers & blues
i can write about dreams and
schemes, living & dying
getting down, losing & grooving
i can write about almost anything—

    but a lonely poem ain't got
no audience
    cause it bleeds all over the page
hits and haunts your face
    hurts your heart as much as your eyes (can you hurt)
a lonely poem ain't about poems
    cause it hurts your heart as much as your eyes
      i say,
oh say
    can you hurt?

    who needs me . . .

Three Legged Chairs

LAMONT B. STEPTOE

make the poem like the hood
couches and three legged chairs
at the curb
scrawled graffiti
on abandoned buildings
fetid damp smell emanating
from dark cellars
two story homes
run down like bad teeth
make the poem like the hood
litter the language with busted wine bottles
scatter old mattresses
people with scrawny cats
color the streetlights blue
have all the trees stagger
like human drunks
let the wind forever sound like gunshots
and sirens
somewhere in all of this children
play and bleed
some escape
on the wings of mother's prayers
some escape
with bullets in the back
some escape
into the church or mental wards
some escape
into bottles and white powders
some escape
at the wheel of the word
some run, jump, dance
into beauty and fame
golden name
most go to graves
embittered, enraged, unknown
and screaming

2.

WHAT IS AFRICA TO ME?

O Daedalus Fly Away Home

ROBERT HAYDEN

Drifting scent of the Georgia pines,
coonskin drum and jubilee banjo:
    pretty Malinda, dance with me.

Night is juba, night is conjo,
    pretty Malinda, dance with me. . . .

Night is an African juju man
weaving a wish and a weariness together
to make two wings.

    O fly away home, fly away

Do you remember Africa?

    O cleave the air, fly away home

I knew all the stars of Africa.

    Spread my wings and cleave the air

My gran, he flew back to Africa,
just spread his arms and flew away home. . . .

Drifting night in the windy pines,
night is a laughing, night is a longing:
    duskrose Malinda, come to me. . . .

Night is a mourning juju man
weaving a wish and a weariness together
to make two wings.

    O fly away home, fly away

Afro-American Fragment

Langston Hughes

So long,
So far away
Is Africa.
Not even memories alive
Save those that history books create,
Save those that songs
Beat back into the blood—
Beat out of blood with words sad-sung
In strange un-Negro tongue—
So long,
So far away
Is Africa.

Subdued and time-lost
Are the drums—and yet
Through some vast mist of race
There comes this song
I do not understand
This song of atavistic land,
Of bitter yearnings lost
Without a place—
So long,
So far away
Is Africa's
Dark face.

O Africa, where I baked my bread

LANCE JEFFERS

O Africa, where I baked my bread
   in the streets at 15 through
   the San Francisco midnights . . .
O Africa, whose San Francisco shouting-church
   on Geary Street and Webster saw a candle
   burning in the middle of my madness . . .
O Africa, whose Fatha Hines and Teddy Wilson
   I took to my piano . . .
O Africa within every brown breast that's suckled me,
   Africa's thousand calmings of my mother-hunger
   across the North American continent . . .
O Africa, within the black folk who've loved me
   in this prelude to the sip-blood time . . .
Africa, I lay my hand upon your swarthy belly—
   and keep it there till death stubs his toe
   against my manhood in the night!

African Dream

Bob Kaufman

In black core of night, it explodes
Silver thunder, rolling back my brain,
Bursting copper screens, memory worlds
Deep in star-fed beds of time,
Seducing my soul to diamond fires of night.
Faint outline, a ship—momentary fright
Lifted on waves of color,
Sunk in pits of light,
Drummed back through time,
Hummed back through mind,
Drumming, cracking the night.
Strange forest songs, skin sounds
Crashing through—no longer strange.
Incestuous yellow flowers tearing
Magic from the earth.
Moon-dipped rituals, led
By a scarlet god,
Caressed by ebony maidens
With daylight eyes,
Purple garments,
Noses that twitch,
Singing young girl songs
Of an ancient love
In dark, sunless places
Where memories are sealed,
Burned in eyes of tigers.
Suddenly wise, I fight the dream:
Green screams enfold my night.

125th Street and Abomey

AUDRE LORDE

Head bent, walking through snow
I see you Seboulisa
printed inside the back of my head
like marks of the newly wrapped akai
that kept my sleep fruitful in Dahomey
and I poured on the red earth in your honor
those ancient parts of me
most precious and least needed
my well-guarded past
the energy-eating secrets
I surrender to you as libation
mother, illuminate my offering
of old victories
over men over women over my selves
who has never before dared
to whistle into the night
take my fear of being alone
like my warrior sisters
who rode in defense of your queendom
disguised and apart
give me the woman strength
of tongue in this cold season.

Half earth and time splits us apart
like struck rock.
A piece lives elegant stories
too simply put
while a dream on the edge of summer
of brown rain in nim trees
snail shells from the dooryard
of King Toffah
bring me where my blood moves
Seboulisa mother goddess with one breast
eaten away by worms of sorrow and loss
see me now
your severed daughter
laughing our name into echo
all the world shall remember.

Song of the Andoumboulou: 8

—maitresse erzulie—

NATHANIEL MACKEY

One hand on her hip, one hand
    arranging her hair,
                blue heaven's
bride. Her beaded hat she hangs
from a nail on the danceroom
              wall. . . .

    As though an angel sought
me out in my sleep or I sat up
    sleepless, eyes like rocks,
             night
like so many such nights I've known.
    Not yet asleep I'm no longer
      awake,   lie awaiting what
stalks the unanswered air,
             still
    awaiting what blunts the running
             flood
or what carries, all Our Mistress's
           whispers,
              thrust
    of a crosscut saw . . .

    Who sits at her feet fills his
    head with wings, oils his
           mouth
    with rum, readies her way
    with perfume . . .
          From whatever glimpse
  of her I get I take heart, I hear them
          say,
    By whatever bit of her I touch
I take
    hold

Outcast

CLAUDE McKAY

For the dim regions whence my fathers came
My spirit, bondaged by the body, longs.
Words felt, but never heard, my lips would frame;
My soul would sing forgotten jungle songs.
I would go back to darkness and to peace,
But the great western world holds me in fee,
And I may never hope for full release
While to its alien gods I bend my knee.
Something in me is lost, forever lost,
Some vital thing has gone out of my heart,
And I must walk the way of life a ghost
Among the sons of earth, a thing apart.

For I was born, far from my native clime,
Under the white man's menace, out of time.

Gift from Kenya

MAY MILLER

Within the day a seventh time
I touch the pale wood antelope.
Forever squat on spindle legs
He tips his head to danger.
(But O to see the pronghorn herd
Run the ridge of a blunted hill
With the skyline copper-red).
It is too late to hear the axe
Which, in the ruined cedar grove,
Shivered down like a death drum note
To fell the trees that would become
The multi-hundred antelopes.

Some fluid centuries ago
My ancient father knew the tree;
Then young and bending in a wind,
Played near the sapling
While the hours of morning whipped
Singing round his loins.
When dark came down and the vultures slept,
In the fragrance of dew-heavy bark
He watched determined stars in course.
As man, in a glittering night of power
He traced with others curving paths
Leading out from the sheltering boughs.

The cedar carved to figurine,
And to all its counterparts,
Is hunched upon the years to come.
The man and his way are old in me,
Old in the unborn who wait
To hold the ice-aged heritage
That has no end in single flesh
However wound in death.

Exploring the Dark Content

HARRYETTE MULLEN

This dream is not a map.
A poem is not the territory.

The dreamer reclines in a barbershop
carpeted with Afro turf.
In the dark some soul yells.

It hurts to walk barefoot
on cowrie shells.

My Father's Geography

AFAA M. WEAVER

I was parading the Côte d'Azur,
hopping the short trains from Nice to Cannes,
following the maze of streets in Monte Carlo
to the hill that overlooks the ville.
A woman fed me pâté in the afternoon,
calling from her stall to offer me more.
At breakfast I talked in French with an old man
about what he loved about America—the Kennedys.

On the beaches I walked and watched
topless women sunbathe and swim,
loving both home and being so far from it.

At a phone looking to Africa over the Mediterranean,
I called my father, and, missing me, he said,
"You almost home boy. Go on cross that sea!"

THE ROCKING LOOM OF HISTORY

Miss Scarlett, Mr. Rhett and Other Latter-Day Saints

MAYA ANGELOU

Novitiates sing Ave
Before the whipping posts,
Criss-crossing their breasts and
tear-stained robes
in the yielding dark.

Animated by the human sacrifice
(Golgotha in black-face)
Priests glow purely white on the
bas-relief of a plantation shrine.

(O Sing)
You are gone but not forgotten
Hail, Scarlett. Requiescat in pace.

God-Makers smear brushes in
blood/gall
to etch frescoes on your
ceilinged tomb.

(O Sing)
Hosanna, King Kotton.

Shadowed couplings of infidels
tempt stigmata from the nipples
of your true-believers.

(Chant Maternoster)
Hallowed Little Eva.

Ministers make novena with the
charred bones of four
very small
very black
very young children

(Intone D I X I E)

And guard the relics
of your intact hymen
daily putting to death,
into eternity,
The stud, his seed,
His seed
His seed.

(O Sing)
Hallelujah, pure Scarlett
Blessed Rhett, the Martyr.

Three Modes of History and Culture

AMIRI BARAKA

Chalk mark sex of the nation, on walls we drummers
know
as cathedrals. Cathedra, in a churning meat milk.

Women glide through looking for telephones. Maps
weep
and are mothers and their daughters listening to

music teachers. From heavy beginnings. Plantations,
learning
America, as speech, and a common emptiness. Songs knocking

inside old women's faces. Knocking through cardboard trunks.
Trains
leaning north, catching hellfire in windows, passing through

the first ignoble cities of missouri, to illinois, and the panting
Chicago.
And then all ways, we go where flesh is cheap. Where factories

sit open, burning the chiefs. Make your way! Up through fog and
history
Make your way, and swing the general, that it come flash open

and spill the innards of that sweet thing we heard, and gave theory
to.
Breech, bridge, and reach, to where all talk is energy. And there's

enough, for anything singular. All our lean prophets and rhythms.
Entire
we arrive and set up shacks, hole cards, Western hearts at the edge

of saying. Thriving to balance the meanness of particular skies.
Race
of madmen and giants.

Brick songs. Shoe songs. Chants of open weariness.
Knife wiggle early evenings of the wet mouth. Tongue
dance midnight, any season shakes our house. Don't
tear my clothes! To doubt the balance of misery

ripping meat hug shuffle fuck. The Party of Insane
Hope, I've come from there too. Where the dead told lies
about clever social justice. Burning coffins voted
and staggered through cold white streets listening
to Willkie or Wallace or Dewey through the dead face
of Lincoln. Come from there, and belched it out.

I think about a time when I will be relaxed.
When flames and non-specific passion wear themselves
away. And my eyes and hands and mind can turn
and soften, and my songs will be softer
and lightly weight the air.

Southern Road

STERLING A. BROWN

Swing dat hammer—hunh—
Steady, bo.
Swing dat hammer—hunh—
Steady, bo;
Ain't no rush, bebby,
Long ways to go.

Burner tore his—hunh—
Black heart away;
Burner tore his—hunh—
Black heart away;
Got me life, bebby,
An' a day.

Gal's on Fifth Street—hunh—
Son done gone;
Gal's on Fifth Street—hunh—
Son done gone;
Wife's in de ward, bebby,
Babe's not bo'n.

My ole man died—hunh—
Cussin' me;
My ole man died—hunh—
Cussin' me;
Ole lady rocks, bebby,
Huh misery.

Doubleshackled—hunh—
Guard behin';
Doubleshackled—hunh—
Guard behin';

Ball an' chain, bebby,
On my min'.

White man tells me—hunh—
Damn yo' soul;
White man tells me—hunh—
Damn yo' soul;
Got no need, bebby,
To be tole.

Chain gang nevah—hunh—
Let me go;
Chain gang nevah—hunh—
Let me go;
Po' los' boy, bebby,
Evahmo' . . .

Tour Guide: La Maison des Esclaves

Ile de Gorée, Senegal

MELVIN DIXON

He speaks of voyages:
men traveling spoon-fashion,
women dying in afterbirth,
babies clinging
to salt-dried nipples.
For what his old eyes still see
his lips have few words. Where
his flat thick feet still walk
his hands crack
into a hundred lifelines.

Here waves rush to shore
breaking news that we return
to empty rooms
where the sea is nothing calm.
And sun, tasting the skin
of black men,
leaves teeth marks.

The rooms are empty until he speaks.
His guttural French is a hawking trader.
His quick Wolof a restless warrior.
His slow, impeccable syllables
a gentleman trader. He tells
in their own language
what they have done.

Our touring maps and cameras ready
we stand in the weighing room
where chained men paraded firm backs,
their women open, full breasts,

and children,
rows of shiny teeth.

Others watched from the balcony,
set the price in guilders, francs,
pesetas and English pounds. Later
when he has finished we too
can leave our coins
where stiff legs dragged
in endless bargain.

He shows how some sat knee-bent
in the first room.
Young virgins waited in the second.
In the third, already red,
the sick and dying
gathered near the exit to the sea.

In the weighing room again
he takes a chain to show us
how it's done. We take
photographs to remember,
others leave coins to forget.
No one speaks
except iron on stone
and the sea
where nothing's safe.

He smiles for he has spoken
of the ancestors: his, ours.
We leave quietly, each alone,
knowing that they who come after us
and breaking
in these tides will find
red empty rooms
to measure long journeys.

The House Slave

Rita Dove

The first horn lifts its arm over the dew-lit grass
and in the slave quarters there is a rustling—
children are bundled into aprons, cornbread

and water gourds grabbed, a salt pork breakfast taken.
I watch them driven into the vague before-dawn
while their mistress sleeps like an ivory toothpick

and Massa dreams of asses, rum and slave-funk.
I cannot fall asleep again. At the second horn,
the whip curls across the backs of the laggards—

sometimes my sister's voice, unmistaken, among them.
"Oh! pray," she cries. "Oh! pray!" Those days
I lie on my cot, shivering in the early heat,

and as the fields unfold to whiteness,
and they spill like bees among the fat flowers,
I weep. It is not yet daylight.

Son of Msippi

HENRY DUMAS

Up
from Msippi I grew.
(Bare walk and cane stalk
make a hungry belly talk.)
Up
from the river of death.
(Walk bare and stalk cane
make a hungry belly talk.)

Up
from Msippi I grew.
Up
from the river of pain.

Out of the long red earth dipping, rising,
spreading out in deltas and plains,
out of the strong black earth turning
over by the iron plough,

out of the swamp green earth dripping
with moss and snakes,

out of the loins of the leveed lands
muscling its American vein:
the great Father of Waters,
I grew
up,
beside the prickly boll of white,
beside the bone-filled Mississippi
rolling on and on,
breaking over,
cutting off,
ignoring my bleeding fingers.

Bare stalk and sun walk
I hear a boll-weevil talk
cause I grew
up
beside the ox and the bow,
beside the rock church and the shack row,
beside the fox and the crow,
beside the melons and maize,
beside the hound dog,
beside the pink hog,
flea-hunting,
mud-grunting,
cat-fishing,
dog pissing
in the Mississippi
rolling on and on,
ignoring the colored coat I spun
of cotton fibers.

Cane-sweat river-boat
nigger-bone floating.

Up from Msippi
I grew,
wailing a song with every strain.

Woman gone woe man too
baby cry rent-pause daddy flew.

(The Recent Past)

C. S. Giscombe

It was the Southern drifting over the flats on a hundred low trestles

and through grade crossings, the city bisected
again & again, this in fact, in memory.

                                        In a dream I stood
in the shadow of one bridge with a boy so coffee-hued I ached
to call him colored to that face as we did each
other as children in Ohio
when we spoke at all.

                              In another it was old diesels
pulling a freight, each one marked THE SOUTHERN
SERVES THE SOUTH, huge white letters
on the dusty sides so I knew where
I was, even dreaming:
                         when the train stopped across a road I climbed up
into the bare ribs of a gondola, how those boys arrived—I knew too—
in Scottsboro,
                    but when we started again
it was a single car trolley through suburbs *up*
on the mountain sd my father, where
the white folks w/ money still live
in Birmingham

                         (not of course a real mountain but boulevards
over high ground,
big houses bespeaking the harmony of all parts

—graceless curiosity stood in for posture in the dream,
myself borne safely through it

Middle Passage

ROBERT HAYDEN

I

Jesús, Estrella, Esperanza, Mercy:

> Sails flashing to the wind like weapons,
> sharks following the moans the fever and the dying;
> horror the corposant and compass rose.

Middle Passage:
>> voyage through death
>>> to life upon these shores.

> "10 April 1800—
> Blacks rebellious. Crew uneasy. Our linguist says
> their moaning is a prayer for death,
> ours and their own. Some try to starve themselves.
> Lost three this morning leaped with crazy laughter
> to the waiting sharks, sang as they went under."

Desire, Adventure, Tartar, Ann:

> Standing to America, bringing home
> black gold, black ivory, black seed.

>> *Deep in the festering hold thy father lies,*
>> *of his bones New England pews are made,*
>> *those are altar lights that were his eyes.*

Jesus   Saviour   Pilot   Me
Over   Life's   Tempestuous   Sea

We pray that Thou wilt grant, O Lord,
safe passage to our vessels bringing
heathen souls unto Thy chastening.

Jesus   Saviour

"8 bells. I cannot sleep, for I am sick
with fear, but writing eases fear a little
since still my eyes can see these words take shape
upon the page & so I write, as one
would turn to exorcism. 4 days scudding,
but now the sea is calm again. Misfortune
follows in our wake like sharks (our grinning
tutelary gods). Which one of us
has killed an albatross? A plague among
our blacks—Ophthalmia: blindness—& we
have jettisoned the blind to no avail.
It spreads, the terrifying sickness spreads.
Its claws have scratched sight from the Capt.'s eyes
& there is blindness in the fo'c'sle
& we must sail 3 weeks before we come
to port."

What port awaits us, Davy Jones'
or home? I've heard of slavers drifting, drifting,
playthings of wind and storm and chance, their crews
gone blind, the jungle hatred
crawling up on deck.

Thou   Who   Walked   On   Galilee

"Deponent further sayeth *The Bella J*
left the Guinea Coast
with cargo of five hundred blacks and odd
for the barracoons of Florida:

"That there was hardly room 'tween-decks for half
the sweltering cattle stowed spoon-fashion there;
that some went mad of thirst and tore their flesh
and sucked the blood:

"That Crew and Captain lusted with the comeliest
of the savage girls kept naked in the cabins;
that there was one they called The Guinea Rose
and they cast lots and fought to lie with her:

"That when the Bo's'n piped all hands, the flames
spreading from starboard already were beyond
control, the negroes howling and their chains
entangled with the flames:

"That the burning blacks could not be reached,
that the Crew abandoned ship,
leaving their shrieking negresses behind,
that the Captain perished drunken with the wenches:

"Further Deponent sayeth not."

Pilot   Oh   Pilot   Me

II

Aye, lad, and I have seen those factories,
Gambia, Rio Pongo, Calabar;
have watched the artful mongos baiting traps
of war wherein the victor and the vanquished

Were caught as prizes for our barracoons.
Have seen the nigger kings whose vanity
and greed turned wild black hides of Fellatah,
Mandingo, Ibo, Kru to gold for us.

And there was one—King Anthracite we named him—
fetish face beneath French parasols
of brass and orange velvet, impudent mouth
whose cups were carven skulls of enemies:

He'd honor us with drum and feast and conjo
and palm-oil-glistening wenches deft in love,
and for tin crowns that shone with paste,
red calico and German-silver trinkets

Would have the drums talk war and send
his warriors to burn the sleeping villages
and kill the sick and old and lead the young
in coffles to our factories.

Twenty years a trader, twenty years,
for there was wealth aplenty to be harvested
from those black fields, and I'd be trading still
but for the fevers melting down my bones.

III

Shuttles in the rocking loom of history,
the dark ships move, the dark ships move,
their bright ironical names
like jests of kindness on a murderer's mouth;
plough through thrashing glister toward
fata morgana's lucent melting shore,
weave toward New World littorals that are
mirage and myth and actual shore.

Voyage through death,
                              voyage whose chartings are unlove.

A charnel stench, effluvium of living death
spreads outward from the hold,
where the living and the dead, the horribly dying,
lie interlocked, lie foul with blood and excrement.

> *Deep in the festering hold thy father lies,*
> *the corpse of mercy rots with him,*
> *rats eat love's rotten gelid eyes.*

> *But, oh, the living look at you*
> *with human eyes whose suffering accuses you,*
> *whose hatred reaches through the swill of dark*
> *to strike you like a leper's claw.*

> *You cannot stare that hatred down*
> *or chain the fear that stalks the watches*
> *and breathes on you its fetid scorching breath;*
> *cannot kill the deep immortal human wish,*
> *the timeless will.*

> "But for the storm that flung up barriers
> of wind and wave, *The Amistad*, señores,
> would have reached the port of Príncipe in two,

46

three days at most; but for the storm we should
have been prepared for what befell.
Swift as the puma's leap it came. There was
that interval of moonless calm filled only
with the water's and the rigging's usual sounds,
then sudden movement, blows and snarling cries
and they had fallen on us with machete
and marlinspike. It was as though the very
air, the night itself were striking us.
Exhausted by the rigors of the storm,
we were no match for them. Our men went down
before the murderous Africans. Our loyal
Celestino ran from below with gun
and lantern and I saw, before the cane-
knife's wounding flash, Cinquez,
that surly brute who calls himself a prince,
directing, urging on the ghastly work.
He hacked the poor mulatto down, and then
he turned on me. The decks were slippery
when daylight finally came. It sickens me
to think of what I saw, of how these apes
threw overboard the butchered bodies of
our men, true Christians all, like so much jetsam.
Enough, enough. The rest is quickly told:
Cinquez was forced to spare the two of us
you see to steer the ship to Africa,
and we like phantoms doomed to rove the sea
voyaged east by day and west by night,
deceiving them, hoping for rescue,
prisoners on our own vessel, till
at length we drifted to the shores of this
your land, America, where we were freed
from our unspeakable misery. Now we
demand, good sirs, the extradition of
Cinquez and his accomplices to La
Havana. And it distresses us to know
there are so many here who seem inclined
to justify the mutiny of these blacks.
We find it paradoxical indeed
that you whose wealth, whose tree of liberty
are rooted in the labor of your slaves

should suffer the august John Quincy Adams
to speak with so much passion of the right
of chattel slaves to kill their lawful masters
and with his Roman rhetoric weave a hero's
garland for Cinquez. I tell you that
we are determined to return to Cuba
with our slaves and there see justice done. Cinquez—
or let us say 'the Prince'—Cinquez shall die."

The deep immortal human wish,
the timeless will:
    Cinquez its deathless primaveral image,
    life that transfigures many lives.

Voyage through death
                to life upon these shores.

Runagate Runagate

ROBERT HAYDEN

I

Runs falls rises stumbles on from darkness into darkness
and the darkness thicketed with shapes of terror
and the hunters pursuing and the hounds pursuing
and the night cold and the night long and the river
to cross and the jack-muh-lanterns beckoning beckoning
and blackness ahead and when shall I reach that somewhere
morning and keep on going and never turn back and keep on going

      Runagate
             Runagate
                   Runagate

Many thousands rise and go
many thousands crossing over

                    O mythic North
                O star-shaped yonder Bible city

Some go weeping and some rejoicing
some in coffins and some in carriages
some in silks and some in shackles

      Rise and go or fare you well

No more auction block for me
no more driver's lash for me

      If you see my Pompey, 30 yrs of age,
      new breeches, plain stockings, negro shoes;
      if you see my Anna, likely young mulatto
      branded E on the right cheek, R on the left,
      catch them if you can and notify subscriber.

Catch them if you can, but it won't be easy.
They'll dart underground when you try to catch them,
plunge into quicksand, whirlpools, mazes,
turn into scorpions when you try to catch them.

And before I'll be a slave
I'll be buried in my grave

North star and bonanza gold
I'm bound for the freedom, freedom-bound
and oh Susyanna don't you cry for me

Runagate

Runagate

II

Rises from their anguish and their power,

Harriet Tubman,

woman of earth, whipscarred,
a summoning, a shining

Mean to be free

And this was the way of it, brethren brethren,
way we journeyed from Can't to Can.
Moon so bright and no place to hide,
the cry up and the patterollers riding,
hound dogs belling in bladed air.
And fear starts a-murbling, Never make it,
we'll never make it. *Hush that now,*
and she's turned upon us, levelled pistol
glinting in the moonlight:
Dead folks can't jaybird-talk, she says;
you keep on going now or die, she says.

Wanted   Harriet Tubman   alias The General
alias Moses   Stealer of Slaves

In league with Garrison   Alcott   Emerson
Garrett   Douglass   Thoreau   John Brown

Armed and known to be Dangerous

Wanted   Reward   Dead or Alive

 Tell me, Ezekiel, oh tell me do you see
 mailed Jehovah coming to deliver me?

Hoot-owl calling in the ghosted air,
five times calling to the hants in the air.
Shadow of a face in the scary leaves,
shadow of a voice in the talking leaves:

 Come ride-a my train

 Oh that train, ghost-story train
 through swamp and savanna movering movering,
 over trestles of dew, through caves of the wish,
 Midnight Special on a sabre track movering movering,
 first stop Mercy and the last Hallelujah.

 Come ride-a my train

  Mean mean mean to be free.

Go Left Out of Shantiville

—"mu" twenty-second part—

Nathaniel Mackey

Say-it-again got hold of us, we
shook. Now neither Paris nor
    Peru was it we were in . . .
                            We
were in Jamaica, St. Ann's Bay, a
        parish peril had to do with, perish
we thought it was we heard. We
heard a music made of swoon, sway.
    Swing had its way with us as
                        well . . .
        An unanswered message on the
machine rewound repeatedly, played
    again, thin balm against what
ravage would come. A sunken isle
                            it
    seemed we lay washed up on,
    adrift on the ythmic, no sooner
    up than gone, dawned on as
                        though
our new day had now come, "mu"
suffusing the otherwise desert air . . .
    In the moving cubicle it arose we
        were in . . . Right sides and
        shoulders, right sides of heads,
                            pressed
    against the window and wall as we
        went left,   pushed by the
bend we rounded, large-arced
            embankment our departure
                        cut . . .

                    Sipped sand, so long without
              water. Lone Coast elixir, mouths
                   drawn shut . . . Euthanasic lip-stitch,
         loquat liqueur,   Oliloquy Valley it

                                            was

                    we came to next . . .   We were
                 each an apocryphal Moses, feet
            newly fitted with sandals, we
               strolled, scrolls long thought to
         be lost unrolled in front of us,

                                      dubbed

                 acoustic scribbling, skanked . . .
            Tumbling water filled my head, I fell
               out laughing, sand so long the one

                                              thing

         met my lip. Two words, *One love,*
                 kept repeating, an asthmatic wuh
            whose we dwelled elsewhere, scattered,
                   worldwide auction block . . .
               Cropped air, coaxed inhalation . . .

                                            Music

                 the breath we took . . . It was only
         there we wanted to be, the everywhere
               we'd always wanted,   ours,

                                         albeit

               only an instant, forever, never to be

                                           heard

         from again

A Hambone Gospel

LAMONT B. STEPTOE

we
a hambone people
we a
gumbo gulosh
we
a gospel feast
of rhythm and rice
bibles and dice
fire and ice
we dark
we black
  blue black
  purple black
  brown black
  yellow black
  yellow brown
  yellow yellow
  red red

we
a hambone people
(we make do)
with boxes and bags
pennies and rags

we out
and way out
we invisible and seen
(know what I mean)
we grow up without green

we right
(and we wrong)

in our get-a-long
we mad
and we bad/sad
we be jubilee

we
a hambone people
we high
and we low
we always on the go
(we movin' too slow)
in our keepin' on keepin' on
we
on time
(don't have much time)
we a passion
we a fashion

we niggers
and nobles
knights and queens
we dancers
and jazzers
singers and saints
prophets and haints
we
a hambone people

Song of the Son

JEAN TOOMER

Pour O pour that parting soul in song,
O pour it in the sawdust glow of night,
Into the velvet pine-smoke air to-night,
And let the valley carry it along.
And let the valley carry it along.

O land and soil, red soil and sweet-gum tree,
So scant of grass, so profligate of pines,
Now just before an epoch's sun declines
Thy son, in time, I have returned to thee,
Thy son, I have in time returned to thee.

In time, for though the sun is setting on
A song-lit race of slaves, it has not set;
Though late, O soil, it is not too late yet
To catch thy plaintive soul, leaving, soon gone,
Leaving, to catch thy plaintive soul soon gone.

O Negro slaves, dark purple ripened plums,
Squeezed, and bursting in the pine-wood air,
Passing, before they stripped the old tree bare
One plum was saved for me, one seed becomes

An everlasting song, a singing tree,
Caroling softly souls of slavery,
What they were, and what they are to me,
Caroling softly souls of slavery.

4.

LIKE WALKING OUT OF SHADOW

In My Father's House

SAMUEL ALLEN

In my father's house when dusk had fallen
I was alone on the dim first floor
I knew there was someone a power intent
On forcing the outer door

How shall I explain—

I bolted it securely
And was locking the inner when
Somehow I was constrained to turn
To see it silently open again

Transfixed before the panther night
My heart gave one tremendous bound
Paralyzed, my feet refused
The intervening ground

—but how shall I say—

I was in the house and dusk had fallen
I was alone on the earthen floor
I *knew* there was a power
Lurking beyond the door

I had bolted the outside—surely
And was closing the inner when

I noticed the first had swung open again
My heart bounded I knew it would be upon me I rushed to the door
It came upon me out of the night and I rushed to the yard
If I could throw the ball the stone the spear in my hand
Against the wall my father would be warned but now
Their hands had fallen on me and they had taken me and I tried
To cry out but O I could not cry out and the cold gray waves
Came over me O stifling me and drowning me . . .

Return of the Native

AMIRI BARAKA

Harlem is vicious
modernism. BangClash.
Vicious the way its made.
Can you stand such beauty?
So violent and transforming.
The trees blink naked, being
so few. The women stare
and are in love with them
selves. The sky sits awake
over us. Screaming
at us. No rain.
Sun, hot cleaning sun
drives us under it.

The place, and place
meant of
black people. Their heavy Egypt.
(Weird word!) Their minds, mine,
the black hope mine. In Time.
We slide along in pain or too
happy. So much love
for us. All over, so much of
what we need. Can you sing
yourself, your life, your place
on the warm planet earth.
And look at the stones

the hearts, the gentle hum
of meaning. Each thing, life
we have, or love, is meant
for us in a world like this.
Where we may see ourselves
all the time. And suffer
in joy, that our lives
are so familiar.

Gordian Knot

CONSTANCE QUARTERMAN BRIDGES

"Great-grandfather Fray was a white man.
He went to another Virginia county to get
grandpa, Albert (his own mixed son) a wife.
He wanted a dark-skin woman because
grandpa looked white." Aunt Edna

Old man Fray always matched his mules
precisely like fitted pieces of a puzzle.
The horses at the mill were perfect pairs.
So it was not too far for him to travel
from his valley over blue mountains
to a distant Virginia county
where Randolph slaves were darker,

with molasses colored Dahomey skin,
African kinked hair and mahogany eyes.
He wanted to untie the weave
of the Gordian Knot, complicated
tangle he had created, with the issue
of silk-haired Albert, his son,
too fair to hide among the varied blacks.

The journey was apology or shame.
But cut or unwoven, the knotted
weave leaves kinks too deep
to hide or smooth away. Great-grandma,
Rhoda, the woman old man Fray found,
opulent with African genes, richly colored
the complex threads of our generations.

We Have Never Loved

SAM CORNISH

we have
never
loved
each other
we
have
only
this house
this street
these neighborhoods
to misunderstand
ourselves
this food
these wages
it is
not love
but
something
deeper
than fear
that makes
you call me
brother
in a strange
city
of white
men

Blackie Thinks of His Brothers

STANLEY CROUCH

They rode north
funky & uneducated
to live
& let themselves rest:

I come here
ghuddammit
to make my way,
lazy or not,
to own myself
open the touch
of my fingers

The southern twang covers
my language & I embarrass
others
I never work
but that is
of others' choice

No one knows my virtues
yet tears split
my flesh &
I say I sweat . . .
Fats Waller added
                    up everything
when the joint was jumpin
"Don't give yo
right name no
No NO"

Blackbottom

TOI DERRICOTTE

When relatives came from out of town,
we would drive down to Blackbottom,
drive slowly down the congested main streets—Beubian and
    Hastings—
trapped in the mesh of Saturday night.
Freshly escaped, black middle class,
we snickered, and were proud;
the louder the streets, the prouder.
We laughed at the bright clothes of a prostitute,
a man sitting on a curb with a bottle in his hand.
We smelled barbecue cooking in dented washtubs, and our mouths
    watered.
As much as we wanted it we couldn't take the chance.
Rhythm and blues came from the windows, the throaty voice of a
    woman lost in the bass, in the drums, in the dirty down and out,
    the grind.
"I love to see a funeral, then I know it ain't mine."
We rolled our windows down so that the waves rolled over us like
    blood.
We hoped to pass invisibly, knowing on Monday we would return
    safely to our jobs, the post office and classroom.
We wanted our sufferings to be offered up as tender meat,
and our triumphs to be belted out in raucous song.
We had lost our voice in the suburbs, in Conant Gardens, where
    each brick house delineated a fence of silence;
we had lost the right to sing in the street and damn creation.

We returned to wash our hands of them,
to smell them
whose very existence
tore us down to the human.

Sorrow Is the Only Faithful One

OWEN DODSON

Sorrow is the only faithful one:
The lone companion clinging like a season
To its original skin no matter what the variations.

If all the mountains paraded
Eating the valleys as they went
And the sun were a cliffure on the highest peak,

Sorrow would be there between
The sparkling and the giant laughter
Of the enemy when the clouds come down to swim.

But I am less, unmagic, black,
Sorrow clings to me more than to doomsday mountains
Or erosion scars on a palisade.

Sorrow has a song like a leech
Crying because the sand's blood is dry
And the stars reflected in the lake
Are water for all their twinkling
And bloodless for all their charm.
I have blood, and a song.
SORROW IS THE ONLY FAITHFUL ONE.

Nigger Song: An Odyssey

RITA DOVE

We six pile in, the engine churning ink:
We ride into the night.
Past factories, past graveyards
And the broken eyes of windows, we ride
Into the gray-green nigger night.

We sweep past excavation sites; the pits
Of gravel gleam like mounds of ice.
Weeds clutch at the wheels;
We laugh and swerve away, veering
Into the black entrails of the earth,
The green smoke sizzling on our tongues . . .

In the nigger night, thick with the smell of cabbages,
Nothing can catch us.
Laughter spills like gin from glasses,
And "yeah" we whisper, "yeah"
We croon, "yeah."

Afro-American

HENRY DUMAS

my black mother birthed me
    my white mother girthed me
my black mother suckled me
    my white mother sucked me in
my black mother sang to me
    my white mother sanctified me
    she crucified me

my black mother is a fine beautiful thang
she bathed me and died for me
she stitched me together, took me into her
bosom and mixed her tears with mine
little black baby i was wretched
a shadow without a body, fatherless, sunless
my black mother shook sweet songs and sweat
all over me and her sugar and her salt saved me

    my white mother is a whore
    with the holy white plague
    a hollow cross between Martha and Mary
    she looked at me and screamed bastard!
    she left me light of body and of mind
    she took what my black mother gave me
    and left me half blind

bone is my black mother
ivory stone
strength is my black mother
my ancient skeletal home
force is my black mother
she maintains and transforms

my black mother is a long-haired sensuous river
where the Kongo flows into the Mississippi she
is coming where my father's blood rises in jets
and like rain, glows, transformed red, tan, black
I am growing in the bosom and in the loins
of America
born and knitted in the soil, when I finish growing
you can pick me up as you would a rare and fabulous
seed and you can
blow Africa
on me as you would a holy reed.

The Wrong Street

CORNELIUS EADY

If you could shuck your skin and watch
The action from a safe vantage point,
You might find a weird beauty in this,
An egoless moment, but for
These young white men at your back.
Your dilemma is how to stay away from
That three to five second shot
On the evening news of the place
Where you stumble, or they catch
Their second wind, or you run up
To the fence, discover that
You are not breeze, or light,
Or a dream that might argue
Itself through the links. Your responsibility
Is not to fall bankrupt, a
Chalk-marked silhouette faintly
Replaying its amazement to
The folks tuning in, fist to
Back, bullet to mid-section.
Your car breaks down
And gives you up. A friend's
Lazy directions miss
The restaurant by two
Important blocks. All of this
Happened. None of this
Happened. Part of this
Happened. (You dream it
After an ordinary day.) Something
Different happened, but now
You run in an
Old story, now you learn
Your name.

Now

CHRISTOPHER GILBERT

I park the car because I'm happy,
because if everyone parked we'd have a street party,
because the moon is full—
it is orange, the sky is closer
and it would be wrong to drive into it.
This is the first day of summer—
everyone is hanging out,
women walk by in their bodies so mellow
I feel I'm near a friend's house.

The small white flakes of the headlights
sweat for a second on the storefronts.
In the windows, darkened afterhours,
a reflection stares back
looking more like me than me.
I reach to touch
and the reflection touches me.
Everything is perfect—
even my skin fits.

Hanging out,
the taillights of the turning cars
are fires, going out—
are the spaces of roses flowered
deeper in themselves. I close my eyes
and am flowered deeper in myself.
Further up the street a walking figure
I can't make out, a face
behind a bag of groceries, free arm swinging
in the air the wave of a deep red
fluid shifting to and fro.

At the vegetarian restaurant
I see it's Michael the Conga Drummer—
been looking for him 2 months.
He asks me, "What's happening."
I love his fingers.
When we shake hands I mix his grip
with the curve of my father's
toting cantelope in the house from the market.
We are two griots at an intersection.
I answer him in parable:
the orange that I've been carrying
is some luminous memory, bursting,
bigger than my hand can hold,
so I hand him half.

Alabama Poem

Nikki Giovanni

if trees could talk
    wonder what they'd say
met an old man
    on the road late afternoon
    hat pulled over to shade
    his eyes
    jacket slumped over his
    shoulders
    told me "girl! my hands seen
    more than all
    them books they got
    at tuskegee"
    smiled at me
    half waved his hand
    walked on down the dusty road
met an old woman
    with a corncob pipe
    sitting and rocking
    on a spring evening
    "sista" she called to me
    "let me tell you—my feet
    seen more than yo eyes
    ever gonna read"
    smiled at her and kept
    on moving
    gave it a thought and went
    back to the porch
    "I say gal" she called down
    "you a student at the institute?
    better come here and study
    these feet
    I'm gonna cut a bunion off
    soons I gets up"
    i looked at her
    she laughed at me
if trees would talk
    wonder what they'd tell me

Tenebris

Angelina Weld Grimké

There is a tree, by day,
That, at night,
Has a shadow,
A hand huge and black,
With fingers long and black.
    All through the dark,
Against the white man's house,
    In the little wind,
The black hand plucks and plucks
    At the bricks.
The bricks are the color of blood and very small.
    Is it a black hand,
    Or is it a shadow?

The Negro Speaks of Rivers

LANGSTON HUGHES

I've known rivers:
I've known rivers ancient as the world and older than the flow of
      human blood in human veins.

My soul has grown deep like the rivers.

I bathed in the Euphrates when dawns were young.
I built my hut near the Congo and it lulled me to sleep.
I looked upon the Nile and raised the pyramids above it.
I heard the singing of the Mississippi when Abe Lincoln went down to
      New Orleans, and I've seen its muddy bosom turn all golden in
      the sunset.

I've known rivers:
Ancient, dusky rivers.

My soul has grown deep like the rivers.

My People

LANGSTON HUGHES

The night is beautiful,
So the faces of my people.

The stars are beautiful,
So the eyes of my people.

Beautiful, also, is the sun.
Beautiful, also, are the souls of my people.

My Blackness Is the Beauty of This Land

LANCE JEFFERS

My blackness is the beauty of this land,
my blackness,
tender and strong, wounded and wise,
my blackness:
I, drawling black grandmother, smile muscular and sweet,
unstraightened white hair soon to grow in earth,
work-thickened hand thoughtful and gentle on grandson's head,
my heart is bloody-razored by a million memories' thrall:

    remembering the crook-necked cracker who spat
        on my naked body,
    remembering the splintering of my son's spirit
        because he remembered to be proud
    remembering the tragic eyes in my daughter's
        dark face when she learned her color's meaning,

and my own dark rage a rusty knife with teeth to gnaw
        my bowels,
my agony ripped loose by anguished shouts in Sunday's
        humble church,
my agony rainbowed to ecstasy when my feet oversoared
        Montgomery's slime,

ah, this hurt, this hate, this ecstasy before I die,
and all my love a strong cathedral!
My blackness is the beauty of this land!

Lay this against my whiteness, this land!
Lay me, young Brutus stamping hard on the cat's tail,
gutting the Indian, gouging the nigger,
booting Little Rock's Minniejean Brown in the buttocks and boast,
    my sharp white teeth derision-bared as I the conqueror crush!

Skyscraper-I, white hands burying God's human clouds beneath
   the dust!
Skyscraper-I, slim blond young Empire
      thrusting up my loveless bayonet to rape the sky,
then shrink all my long body with filth and in the gutter lie
as lie I will to perfume this armpit garbage,
While I here standing black beside
wrench tears from which the lies would suck the salt
to make me more American than America . . .
But yet my love and yet my hate shall civilize this land,
this land's salvation.

The Bones of My Father

ETHERIDGE KNIGHT

1

There are no dry bones
here in this valley. The skull
of my father grins
at the Mississippi moon
from the bottom
of the Tallahatchie,
the bones of my father
are buried in the mud
of these creeks and brooks that twist
and flow their secrets to the sea.
but the wind sings to me
here the sun speaks to me
of the dry bones of my father.

2

There are no dry bones
in the northern valleys, in the Harlem alleys
young/black/men with knees bent
nod on the stoops of the tenements
and dream
of the dry bones of my father.

And young white longhairs who flee
their homes, and bend their minds
and sing their songs of brotherhood
and no more wars are searching for
my father's bones

3

There are no dry bones here.
We hide from the sun.
No more do we take the long straight strides.

Our steps have been shaped by the cages
that kept us. We glide sideways
like crabs across the sand.
We perch on green lilies, we search
beneath white rocks . . .
THERE ARE NO DRY BONES HERE

The skull of my father
grins at the Mississippi moon
from the bottom
of the Tallahatchie.

How I See Things

Yusef Komunyakaa

I hear you were
sprawled on the cover of *Newsweek*
with freedom marchers, those years
when blood tinted the photographs,
when fire leaped into the trees.

Negatives of nightriders
develop in the brain.
The Strawberry Festival Queen
waves her silk handkerchief,
executing a fancy high kick

flashback through the heart.
Pickups with plastic Jesuses
on dashboards head for hoedowns.
Men run twelve miles into wet cypress
swinging bellropes. Ignis fatuus can't be blamed

for the charred Johnson grass.
Have we earned the right
to forget, forgive
ropes for holding
to moonstruck branches?

Every last stolen whisper
the hoot owl echoes
turns leaves scarlet.
Hush shakes the monkeypod
till pink petal-tongues fall.

You're home in New York.
I'm back here in Bogalusa
with one foot in pinewoods.

The mockingbird's blue note
sounds to me like *please*,

please. A beaten song
threaded through the skull
by cross hairs.
Black hands still turn blood red
working the strawberry fields.

The Question of Identity

KRISTIN LATTANY

The Danes all told my husband, "Your French wife
Is charming," and in slyer, suaver France,
Above, below the flow of café life,
The Question shimmered, shadowed. "Will you dance
A temple dance for us?"—Like Prophet Jones,
Shuffling to tambourines and happy groans?

In London I was from Bombay; again
In Paris, I found I could not faze
By answering, "Je suis Americaine,"
Those who demanded, "Etes-vous japonnaise?"
No matter what I said, they smiled. They knew.
"Vous êtes de Guadeloupe. Ou de Peru."

From clutching, claiming, sungilt, spice-stained hands,
I fled through every boulevard and bar,
Denying all their dim, exotic lands,
Repeating, firmly, clearly, "Je suis noire."
—Accused of Ecuador and Pakistan,
I closed my atlas, packed my bags, and ran

To Venice and her Byzantine bazaars.
There, seeing, serving, robbing everyone,
They asked me no more than they would the stars.
I was nothing new beneath the sun
Where down the dark canals, past gilded doors,
Had glided Turks, Assyrians and Moors.

And there beneath a slightly pointed dome
Received the benediction of a saint
Whose calm ambiguous features were at home
In all of earth and heaven. *They* could paint
The martyrdom of living with a face
Whose only label was the human race.

The Black Unicorn

Audre Lorde

The black unicorn is greedy.
The black unicorn is impatient.
The black unicorn was mistaken
for a shadow
or symbol
and taken
through a cold country
where mist painted mockeries
of my fury.
It is not on her lap where the horn rests
but deep in her moonpit
growing.

The black unicorn is restless
the black unicorn is unrelenting
the black unicorn is not
free.

Song of the Andoumboulou: 12

NATHANIEL MACKEY

Weathered raft I saw myself
adrift on.

Battered wood I dreamt I
drummed on, driven.

Scissored rose, newly braided
   light, slack hoped-for rope
      groped at, unraveled.
                        Braided star
we no longer saw but remembered,
    threads overlapping the rim
of a sunken world, rocks we
    no longer saw by extinguished,
Namoratunga's long-tethered
                            light.

Breathing smoke left by the gods'
exit. Scorched earth looked at
with outside eyes, burnt leaf's
                  Osanyin,
    raffia straw beneath
    coatings of camwood
                paste . . .

Saw myself bled, belatedly
   cut, inverted blade
   atop Eshu's head,
               sawtooth
cloth of an egungun,
   thunder whet the edge
             of a knife.

And what love had to do with it
   stuttered, bit its tongue.
    Bided our time, said only wait,
                              we'd see.

Tossed-off covers.   King Sunny Adé's
wet brow.   Four twenties on the dresser
   by the bed . . .

    Cramped egg we might work our
  way out of,   caress reaching in
   to the bones underneath.
                       Not even
looking. Even so, see
             thru.

Watery light we tried in vain
   to pull away from.   Painted
                    face,
disembodied voice. Dramas we
   wooed, invited in but got
scared of.   Song so black it
               burnt
my lip . . .   Tore my throat as I
  walked up Real Street. Raw beginner,
                         green
  attempt to sing the blues . . .

Tilted sky, turned earth. Bent wheel, burnt
                  we.
   Bound I. Insubordinate
           us

Swallow the Lake

Clarence Major

Gave me things I
could not use. Then. Now.
Rain night bursting upon & into. I
shine updown into Lake Michigan.

like the glow from the cold lights of the Loop.
Walks. Deaths. Births.
Streets. Things I could not give back. Nor
use. Or night or day or night or

loneliness. Other ways   feelings I could not
put into words   into themselves into people.
Blank monkeys of the hierarchy. More deaths—
stupidity & death turning them on

into the beat of my droopy heart   my middle
passage blues my corroding hate my release
while I come to become neon iron eyes stainless lungs
blood zincgripped steel I
come up abstract

not able to take their bricks. Tar. Nor their flesh.
I ran: stung. Loop fumes hung
                              in my smoky lungs.

ideas I could not break nor form. Gave me
things I
see break & run down the crawling down the
game.

Illusion illusion, and you
would swear before screaming somehow
choked voices in me.

The crawling thing in the blood, the
huge immune loneliness. One becomes immune
to the bricks the feelings. One becomes
death.
One becomes each one and every person I
become. I could not
I COULD NOT
I could not whistle and walk in storms
along Lake Michigan's shore. Concrete walks.
I could not swallow the lake

The Griots Who Know Brer Fox

COLLEEN J. MCELROY

There are old drunks among the tenements,
old men who have been
                              lost
forever from families, shopping centers
starched shirts and
                              birthdays.
They are the griots, the story tellers
whose faces are knotted and swollen
               into a black patchwork
               of open sores and
               old scabs; disease
               transforms the nose
               into cabbage   the eyes
               are dried egg yolks.
They grind old tobacco between scabby gums
like ancient scarabs rolling dung from tombs
in their
                              mother country.
In this country, they are scenic, part of the
view from Route 1, Old Town.

Don't miss them; they sit in doorways
of boarded houses in the part of town
nestled between wide roads named for
English kings and tourists.
               These old men sit like moldy stumps
               among the broken bricks of narrow
               carriage streets, streets paved
               with the Spirits of '76,
               the Westward Movement and Oz.

These old men never travel the wide roads;
they sit in the dusk, dark skinned as Aesop,

remember their youth. They chant stories
to keep themselves awake another day;
                tales of girls bathing in kitchens
                before wood stoves, smells of
                        the old South.
                Or Northern tales of babies bitten
                by rats, women who've left them
                or how they were once rich.
They'll spin a new Brer Rabbit story for a nickel;
tell you how he slipped past the whistle-slick fox
to become
                the Abomey king.
But you must listen closely,
it moves fast, their story
skipping and jumping childlike;
the moral hidden in an enchanted forest
                        of word games.
                These stories are priceless,
                prized by movie moguls
                who dream of Saturday matinees
                and full houses.
You have to look beyond the old men's faces,
beyond the rat that waits to nibble the hand
when they sleep. The face is anonymous,
                        you can find it anywhere
but the words are as prized
as the curved tusks of the bull elephant.

Black Power

RAYMOND PATTERSON

I stepped from black to black.
It was so simply done—
Like walking out of shadow
And going forth in sun—
And I will not look back.

But if you ask me how
That day was, what I saw,
These memories linger now:
An easing at the core,
A clearer sense of what
I am, a keener taste
For life; the urge to touch
My shining hands and face—
And marvel at how much
They please me in each case.

Still one of Nature's creatures;
Yet my own self; content
With all my inner features,
The knowledge I was meant
To give them liberty.

What passed was slavery—
Of giving hatred back,
Of hating to be free
Of what turned black in me
Through tortured history.

What sense can words convey
Of what it was I saw?
. . . The weather of that day,
The pain I knew before
Without once looking back
I stepped from black to black?

Blue

CARL PHILLIPS

As through marble or the lining of
certain fish split open and scooped
clean, this is the blue vein
that rides, where the flesh is even
whiter than the rest of her, the splayed
thighs mother forgets, busy struggling
for command over bones: her own,
those of the chaise longue, all
equally uncooperative, and there's
the wind, too. This is her hair, gone
from white to blue in the air.

This is the black, shot with blue, of my dark
daddy's knuckles, that do not change, ever.
Which is to say they are no more pale
in anger than at rest, or when, as
I imagine them now, they follow
the same two fingers he has always used
to make the rim of every empty blue
glass in the house sing.
Always, the same
blue-to-black sorrow
no black surface can entirely hide.

Under the night, somewhere
between the white that is nothing so much as
blue, and the black that is, finally, nothing,
I am the man neither of you remembers.
Shielding, in the half-dark,
the blue eyes I sometimes forget
I don't have. Pulling my own stoop-
shouldered kind of blues across paper.
Apparently misinformed about the rumored
stuff of dreams: everywhere I inquired,
I was told look for blue.

Ballad of Black/Essence

For Joseph Harrison

EUGENE B. REDMOND

Firstforce or earth-driven godman; globe-song:
        Dance-embroidered in rhythmtree;
Flamefever inside blood, inside raindrops;
        Phone-song from a phono-sea.

Drumgirl, horizon-child: sprite moondancer!
        Fleshtorch, essence and *jewelskin*:
Comming/coming strongsong, blues-laced and black:
        Deftly making words out of wind.

Landlaced man, mud-docked and *waterwavy*,
        Oh *steel* that walks, that swims, that *flies!*
Softstone with armor to endure: to lure;
        Flowers inside iron: inside eyes!

Fleet/force, redemptive strength, precious muscle:
        Essence, the blackline and the core:
Beauty   /yes/   vim-vexed and *fire within fire*
        That *flares up!* frames and fans the shore:

That *flares up!* enflames the shore of seacoals;
        Giving and summoning the seed
Of light, sun, flamedances on rockshoulders:
        Burning and branding in our need;
        Burning and branding in our need.

Flounder

NATASHA TRETHEWEY

Here, she said, *put this on your head.*
She handed me a hat.
You 'bout as white as your dad,
and you gone stay like that.

Aunt Sugar rolled her nylons down
around each bony ankle,
and I rolled down my white knee socks
letting my thin legs dangle,

circling them just above water
and silver backs of minnows
flitting here then there between
the sun spots and the shadows.

This is how you hold the pole
to cast the line out straight.
Now put that worm on your hook,
throw it out and wait.

She sat spitting tobacco juice
into a coffee cup.
Hunkered down when she felt the bite,
jerked the pole straight up

reeling and tugging hard at the fish
that wriggled and tried to fight back.
A flounder, she said, and *you can tell*
'cause one of its sides is black.

The other side is white, she said.
It landed with a thump.
I stood there watching that fish flip-flop,
switch sides with every jump.

For My People

MARGARET WALKER

For my people everywhere singing their slave songs repeatedly: their
dirges and their ditties and their blues and jubilees, praying their
prayers nightly to an unknown god, bending their knees humbly
to an unseen power;

For my people lending their strength to the years, to the gone years
and the now years and the maybe years, washing ironing cook-
ing scrubbing sewing mending hoeing plowing digging planting
pruning patching dragging along never gaining never reaping
never knowing and never understanding;

For my playmates in the clay and dust and sand of Alabama backyards
playing baptizing and preaching and doctor and jail and soldier
and school and mama and cooking and playhouse and concert
and store and hair and Miss Choomby and company;

For the cramped bewildered years we went to school to learn to know
the reasons why and the answers to and the people who and the
places where and the days when, in memory of the bitter hours
when we discovered we were black and poor and small and dif-
ferent and nobody cared and nobody wondered and nobody un-
derstood;

For the boys and girls who grew in spite of these things to be man
and woman, to laugh and dance and sing and play and drink
their wine and religion and success, to marry their playmates
and bear children and then die of consumption and anemia and
lynching;

For my people thronging 47th Street in Chicago and Lenox Avenue in
New York and Rampart Street in New Orleans, lost disinherited
dispossessed and happy people filling the cabarets and taverns
and other people's pockets needing bread and shoes and milk
and land and money and something—something all our own;

For my people walking blindly spreading joy, losing time being lazy, sleeping when hungry, shouting when burdened, drinking when hopeless, tied and shackled and tangled among ourselves by the unseen creatures who tower over us omnisciently and laugh;

For my people blundering and groping and floundering in the dark of churches and schools and clubs and societies, associations and councils and committees and conventions, distressed and disturbed and deceived and devoured by money-hungry glory-craving leeches, preyed on by facile force of state and fad and novelty, by false prophet and holy believer;

For my people standing staring trying to fashion a better way from confusion, from hypocrisy and misunderstanding, trying to fashion a world that will hold all the people, all the faces, all the adams and eves and their countless generations;

Let a new earth rise. Let another world be born. Let a bloody peace be written in the sky. Let a second generation full of courage issue forth; let a people loving freedom come to growth. Let a beauty full of healing and a strength of final clenching be the pulsing in our spirits and our blood. Let the martial songs be written, let the dirges disappear. Let a race of men now rise and take control.

5

IF WE MUST DIE

Poem for Halfwhite College Students

AMIRI BARAKA

Who are you, listening to me, who are you
listening to yourself? Are you white or
black, or does that have anything to do
with it? Can you pop your fingers to no
music, except those wild monkies go on
in your head, can you jerk, to no melody,
except finger poppers get it together
when you turn from starchecking to checking
yourself. How do you sound, your words, are they
yours? The ghost you see in the mirror, is it really
you, can you swear you are not an imitation grayboy,
can you look right next to you in that chair, and swear,
that the sister you have your hand on is not really
so full of Elizabeth Taylor, Richard Burton is
coming out of her ears. You may even have to be Richard
with a white shirt and face, and four million negroes
think you cute, you may have to be Elizabeth Taylor, old lady,
if you want to sit up in your crazy spot dreaming about dresses,
and the sway of certain porters' hips. Check yourself, learn who it is
speaking, when you make some ultrasophisticated point, check
    yourself,
when you find yourself gesturing like Steve McQueen, check it out, ask
in your black heart who it is you are, and is that image black or white,

you might be surprised right out the window, whistling dixie on the
    way in.

Beverly Hills, Chicago

"and the people live till they have white hair"
—E. M. Price

GWENDOLYN BROOKS

The dry brown coughing beneath their feet,
(Only a while, for the handyman is on his way)
These people walk their golden gardens.
We say ourselves fortunate to be driving by today.

That we may look at them, in their gardens where
The summer ripeness rots. But not raggedly.
Even the leaves fall down in lovelier patterns here.
And the refuse, the refuse is a neat brilliancy.

When they flow sweetly into their houses
With softness and slowness touched by that everlasting gold,
We know what they go to. To tea. But that does not mean
They will throw some little black dots into some water and add sugar
    and the juice of the cheapest lemons that are sold,

While downstairs that woman's vague phonograph bleats, "Knock me
    a kiss."
And the living all to be made again in the sweatingest physical manner
Tomorrow. . . . Not that anybody is saying that these people have no
    trouble.
Merely that it is trouble with a gold-flecked beautiful banner.

Nobody is saying that these people do not ultimately cease to be. And
Sometimes their passings are even more painful than ours.
It is just that so often they live till their hair is white.
They make excellent corpses, among the expensive flowers. . . .

Nobody is furious. Nobody hates these people.
At least, nobody driving by in this car.

It is only natural, however, that is should occur to us
How much more fortunate they are than we are.

It is only natural that we should look and look
At their wood and brick and stone
And think, while a breath of pine blows,
How different these are from our own.

We do not want them to have less.
But it is only natural that we should think we have not enough.
We drive on, we drive on.
When we speak to each other our voices are a little gruff.

the ISM

WANDA COLEMAN

tired i count the ways in which it determines my life
permeates everything. it's in the air
lives next door to me in stares of neighbors
meets me each day in the office. its music comes out the radio
drives beside me in my car. strolls along with me
down supermarket aisles
it's on television
and in the streets even when my walk is casual/undefined
it's overhead flashing lights
i find it in my mouth
when i would speak of other things

Death of Dr. King

SAM CORNISH

#1
we sit outside
the bars   the dime stores
everything is closed today

we are mourning
our hands filled with bricks
a brother is dead

my eyes are white and cold
water is in my hands

this is grief

#2
after the water
the broken bread
we return
to our separate
places

in our heads
bodies collapse
and grow again

the city boils
black men
jump out of trees

Is It Because I Am Black?

Joseph Seamon Cotter Jr.

Why do men smile when I speak,
And call my speech
The whimperings of a babe
That cries but knows not what it wants?
Is it because I am black?

Why do men sneer when I arise
And stand in their councils,
And look them eye to eye,
And speak their tongue?
Is it because I am black?

Homestead, USA

D. L. CROCKETT-SMITH

Along the cracked seams of Wall Street, the poor
multiply, evicted from slums and psych
wards. A gaunt new disease sucks
the marrow from men's bones.

Is there no cure for this sickness
that flushes citizens into the gutters?
We peer through the iron bars around the White House.
The bankers clutch their squash rackets.
The guards clutch their guns.

Women sleep on steam vents,
lives shoved in shopping bags.
Men feast like rats on fresh garbage.
O pioneers, who settle this new frontier!

A Litany at Atlanta

Done at Atlanta,
in the Day of Death, 1906

W. E. B. DuBois

O Silent God, Thou whose voice afar in mist and mystery hath left our ears an-hungered in these fearful days—
Hear us, good Lord!

Listen to us, Thy children: our faces dark with doubt are made a mockery in Thy sanctuary. With uplifted hands we front Thy heaven, O God crying:
We beseech Thee to hear us, good Lord!

We are not better than our fellows, Lord, we are but weak and human men. When our devils do deviltry, curse Thou the doer and the deed: curse them as we curse them, do to them all and more than ever they have done to innocence and weakness, to womanhood and home.
Have mercy upon us, miserable sinners!

And yet whose is the deeper guilt? Who made these devils? Who nursed them in crime and fed them on injustice? Who ravished and debauched their mothers and their grandmothers? Who bought and sold their crime, and waxed fat and rich on public iniquity?
Thou knowest, good God!

Is this Thy Justice, O Father, that guile be easier than innocence, and the innocent crucified for the guilt of the untouched guilty?
Justice, O Judge of men!

Wherefore do we pray? Is not the God of the fathers dead? Have not seers seen in Heaven's halls Thine hearsed and lifeless form stark amidst the black and rolling smoke of sin, where all along bow bitter forms of endless dead?
Awake, Thou that sleepest!

Thou are not dead, but flown afar, up hills of endless light, thru blazing corridors of suns, where worlds do swing of good and gentle men, of women strong and free—far from the cozenage, black hypocrisy and chaste prostitution of this shameful speck of dust!

Turn again, O Lord, leave us not to perish in our sin!

From lust of body and lust of blood
Great God, deliver us!

From lust of power and lust of gold,
Great God, deliver us!

From the leagued lying of despot and of brute,
Great God, deliver us!

A city lay in travail, God our Lord, and from her loins sprang twin Murder and Black Hate. Red was the midnight; clang, crack and cry of death and fury filled the air and trembled underneath the stars when church spires pointed silently to Thee. And all this was to sate the greed of greedy men who hide behind the veil of vengeance!

Bend us Thine ear, O Lord!

In the pale, still morning we looked upon the deed. We stopped our ears and held our leaping hands, but they—did they not wag their heads and leer and cry with bloody jaws: *Cease from Crime!* The word was mockery, for thus they train a hundred crimes while we do cure one.

Turn again our captivity, O Lord!

Behold this maimed and broken thing; dear God, it was an humble black man who toiled and sweat to save a bit from the pittance paid him. They told him: *Work and Rise.* He worked. Did this man sin? Nay, but some one told how some one said another did—one whom he had never seen nor known. Yet for that man's crime this man lieth maimed and murdered, his wife naked to shame, his children, to poverty and evil.

Hear us, O Heavenly Father!

Doth not this justice of hell stink in Thy nostrils, O God? How long shall the mounting flood of innocent blood roar in Thine ears and pound in our hearts for vengeance? Pile the pale frenzy of blood-crazed brutes who do such deeds high on Thine altar, Jehovah Jireh, and burn it in hell forever and forever!

Forgive us, good Lord; we know not what we say!

Bewildered we are, and passion-tost, mad with the madness of a mobbed and mocked and murdered people; straining at the armposts of Thy Throne, we raise our shackled hands and charge Thee, God, by the bones of our stolen fathers, by the tears of our dead mothers, by the very blood of Thy crucified Christ: *What meaneth this?* Tell us the Plan; give us the Sign!
Keep not Thou silence, O God!

Sit no longer blind, Lord God, deaf to our prayer and dumb to our dumb suffering. Surely, Thou too art not white, O Lord, a pale, bloodless, heartless thing?
Ah! Christ of all the Pities!

Forgive the thought! Forgive these wild, blasphemous words. Thou art still the God of our black fathers, and in Thy soul's soul sit some soft darkenings of the evening, some shadowings of the velvet night.

But whisper—speak—call, great God, for Thy silence is white terror to our hearts! The way, O God, show us the way and point us the path.

Whither? North is greed and South is blood; within, the coward, and without the liar. Whither? To death?
Amen! Welcome dark sleep!

Whither? To life? But not this life, dear God, not this. Let the cup pass from us, tempt us not beyond our strength, for there is that clamoring and clawing within, to whose voice we would not listen, yet shudder lest we must, and it is red, Ah! God! It is a red and awful shape.
Selah!

In yonder East trembles a star.
Vengeance is mine; I will repay, saith the Lord!

Thy will, O Lord, be done!
Kyrie Eleison!

Lord, we have done these pleading, wavering words.
We beseech Thee to hear us, good Lord!

We bow our heads and hearken soft to the sobbing of women and little children.
We beseech Thee to hear us, good Lord!

Our voices sink in silence and in night.
Hear us, good Lord!

In night, O God of a godless land!
Amen!

In silence, O Silent God.
Selah!

America

HENRY DUMAS

If an eagle be imprisoned
On the back of a coin
And the coin is tossed into the sky,
That coin will spin,
That coin will flutter,
But the eagle will never fly.

We Wear the Mask

Paul Laurence Dunbar

We wear the mask that grins and lies,
It hides our cheeks and shades our eyes,—
This debt we pay to human guile;
With torn and bleeding hearts we smile,
And mouth with myriad subtleties.

Why should the world be overwise,
In counting all our tears and sighs?
Nay, let them only see us, while
   We wear the mask.

We smile, but, O great Christ, our cries
To thee from tortured souls arise.
We sing, but oh the clay is vile
Beneath our feet, and long the mile;
But let the world dream otherwise,
   We wear the mask!

The World I See

Mari Evans

There is no beauty
to the world I see
save moments stopped in
Time
preserved
in
unreality . . .
Blood from the streets
from the dim bayou
surges
and the river of it
clouds
my view till hate
with an incandescent hue
purges
what was love
burns me
free
. . . of you
There are no birds
no sky
no sea and
only hate
stares back
at me
Where . . .
is the music
I would feel . . .
I hear no song.
. . . just my hate
is real . . .

Night, Death, Mississippi

ROBERT HAYDEN

I

A quavering cry. Screech-owl?
Or one of them?
The old man in his reek
and gauntness laughs—

One of them, I bet—
and turns out the kitchen lamp,
limping to the porch to listen
in the windowless night.

Be there with Boy and the rest
if I was well again.
Time was. Time was.
White robes like moonlight.

In the sweetgum dark.
Unbucked that one then
and him squealing bloody Jesus
as we cut it off.

Time was. A cry?
A cry all right.
He hawks and spits,
fevered as by groinfire.

Have us a bottle,
Boy and me—
he's earned him a bottle—
when he gets home.

II

Then we beat them, he said,
beat them till our arms was tired

and the big old chains
messy and red.

O Jesus burning on the lily cross

Christ, it was better
than hunting bear
which don't know why
you want him dead.

O night, rawhead and bloodybones night

You kids fetch Paw
some water now so's he
can wash that blood
off him, she said.

O night betrayed by darkness not its own

The Mob

Calvin Hernton

Summer sets on the cities like a hen
On a package with a ticking noise inside—
New York, Chicago, Birmingham,
Newark, Atlanta, Watts . . .

The sun is on fire.

We rise and go forth
Flesh withering, bones tinkling,
Tottering, we
Brace ourselves alone
Against stone
Protoplasm against steel
Rigid before the loneliness in
The other's skin.

Fire tongued to dead ears
Wintered selves
Digging graves in summertime.

There is something dreadful
About our being here this way, undulating
In the streets,
Blasted down, flesh scorched by liquid rays
Of baptismal hose,
Something abandoned, fetching
At the worm in the rock of our fists,
Something in the breast
Which the heart cannot
Or dare not utter.

When
If at last we meet

In death-threaded exigence
It is no accident we scream obscenity—
All our life is obscenity
There is nothing accidental about trash.

The sun also screams.

Ravished the sky, the junkyard,
The citied streets,
Forlorn we limp away:
Head helmets,
Body bayonets,
Bloody rags.

Dream Boogie

Langston Hughes

Good morning, daddy!
Ain't you heard
The boogie-woogie rumble
Of a dream deferred?

Listen closely:
You'll hear their feet
Beating out and beating out a—

> *You think*
> *It's a happy beat?*

Listen to it closely:
Ain't you heard
something underneath
like a—

> *What did I say?*

Sure,
I'm happy!
Take it away!

> *Hey, pop!*
> *Re-bop!*
> *Mop!*

> *Y-e-a-h!*

Tired

FENTON JOHNSON

I am tired of work; I am tired of building up somebody else's
      civilization.
Let us take a rest, M'Lissy Jane.
I will go down to the Last Chance Saloon, drink a gallon or two of
      gin, shoot a game or two of dice and sleep the rest of the night
      on one of Mike's barrels.
You will let the old shanty go to rot, the white people's clothes turn to
      dust, and the Calvary Baptist Church sink to the bottomless pit.
You will spend your days forgetting you married me and your nights
      hunting the warm gin Mike serves the ladies in the rear of the
      Last Chance Saloon.
Throw the children into the river; civilization has given us too many.
      It is better to die than to grow up and find that you are colored.
Pluck the stars out of the heavens. The stars mark our destiny. The
      stars marked my destiny.
I am tired of civilization.

If We Must Die

CLAUDE MCKAY

If we must die, let it not be like hogs
Hunted and penned in an inglorious spot,
While round us bark the mad and hungry dogs,
Making their mock at our accursed lot.
If we must die, O let us nobly die,
So that our precious blood may not be shed
In vain; then even the monsters we defy
Shall be constrained to honor us though dead!
O kinsmen! we must meet the common foe!
Though far outnumbered let us show us brave,
And for their thousand blows deal one deathblow!
What though before us lies the open grave?
Like men we'll face the murderous, cowardly pack,
Pressed to the wall, dying, but fighting back!

Watts

CONRAD KENT RIVERS

Must I shoot the
white man dead
to free the nigger
in his head?

Walk Like Freedom

Carolyn Rodgers

she turned to me
and said
the weather's bad, isn't it?
and underneath it all
i heard her saying
i'm white and
we run
the world.

the train can't be late,
he said
i have a business appointment to keep
in only 40 minutes/the train must not be late.
and underneath it all he was
clearly saying
i'm white and i/we
run
the world.

they stand around sometimes
with their faces stolid and impassive
no smiles or frowns
the sum total of often exchanges
just them saying
with/or without words—

we're white
and
we run
the world.

how
do we

dare/we must
go on

we dare to
walk the ways of freedom.

A Poem for Players

AL YOUNG

Yes, theyll let you play,
let you play third base or fender bass,
let you play Harrah's Club or Shea Stadium

Theyll let you play
in a play anyway: Shakespeare,
Ionesco, Bullins, Baraka, or Genet,
only dont get down *too* much
& dont go gettin too uppity

Theyll let you play,
oh yes, on the radio, stereo,
even on the video, Ojays,
O.J. Simpson, only please dont stray
too far from your ghetto rodeo

Theyll let you be Satchmo,
theyll let you be Diz,
theyll let you be Romeo,
    or star in *The Wiz*
but you gots to remember that
    that's all there is

Oh, you can be a lawyer or a medico,
a well-briefcased executive with Texaco;
you can even get yourself hired, man,
to go teach *Ulysses* in Dublin, Ireland

Theyll let you play
so long as you dont play around,
so long as you play it hot or cool,
so long as you dont play down the blues

theyll let you play in *Playboy, Playgirl,*
    or the *Amsterdam News*

Finally theyll let you play
politics if you dont get in the way
the way some of us did and had to be
iced by conspiracy, international mystery

Theyll let you play anybody but you,
that's pretty much what they will do

6.

THIS MAN SHALL BE REMEMBERED

Robeson at Rutgers

ELIZABETH ALEXANDER

Hard to picture, but these Goliath trees
are taller still than Robeson. Outside
vast plate windows in this lecture hall,
I imagine him running down autumn fields,
see his black thighs pumping that machinery
across chalk-painted lines.

                    He loved the woman
in the lab, Eslanda, who saw order
in swimming circles on inch-wide slides, who
made photographs. I picture her standing
in darkness, led by red light, bathing paper
in broth, extracting images. Did this woman smile
to watch white paper darken, to pull wet
from the chemicals Paul Robeson's totem face?

American Gothic

To Satch
(The legendary Satchell Paige, one of the star pitchers in Negro baseball)

SAMUEL ALLEN

Sometimes I feel like I will *never* stop
Just go on forever
Til one fine mornin'
I'm gonna reach up and grab me a handfulla stars
Swing out my long lean leg
And whip three hot strikes burnin' down the heavens
And look over at God and say
How about that!

For Malcolm: After Mecca

My whole life has been a chronology of—changes.

GERALD BARRAX

You lie now in many coffins
in parlors where your name
is dropped more heavily even than Death
sent you crashing to the stage
on which you had exorcised our shame.

In little rooms they gather now
bringing their own memories of your pilgrimage
they come and go
speaking of revolution
without knowing as you learned
how static hate is
without recognizing the man you were
lay in our shame
and your growth into martyrdom.

Music for Martyrs

Steve Biko, killed in South Afrika for loving his people

GWENDOLYN BROOKS

I feel a regret, Steve Biko.
I am sorry, Steve Biko.
    Biko the Emerger
laid low.

Now for the shapely American memorials.
The polished tears.
The timed tempest.
The one-penny poems.
The hollow guitars.
The joke oh jaunty.
The vigorous veal-stuffed voices.
The singings, the white lean lasses with streaming
yellow hair.
Now for the organized nothings.
Now for the weep-words.

Now for the rigid recountings
of your tracts, your triumphs, your tribulations.

Malcolm X

Gwendolyn Brooks

Original.
Ragged-round.
Rich-robust.

He had the hawk-man's eyes.
We gasped. We saw the maleness.
The maleness raking out and making guttural the air
and pushing us to walls.

And in a soft and fundamental hour
a sorcery devout and vertical
beguiled the world.

He opened us—
who was a key,

who was a man.

harriet

LUCILLE CLIFTON

harriet
if i be you
let me not forget
to be the pistol
pointed
to be the madwoman
at the rivers edge
warning
be free or die
and isabell
if i be you
let me in my
sojourning
not forget
to ask my brothers
ain't i a woman too
and
grandmother
if i be you
let me not forget to
work hard
trust the Gods
love my children and
wait.

Harriet Tubman

SAM CORNISH

1

Lord, while I sow earth or song
the sun goes down. My only mother
on a dirt floor is dying, her
mouth open on straw and black
soil, the smell of stew or chicken
in a pot her only memories. I think
of the children
                  made in her and sold.

Dry hair falling from her skull,
she moves when my silent feet
come in from the fields. I think
she knows I live her life. What
passes from the mother kills the child
before death.
Lord, you hide behind books
and words.
                      I sing to hide
the sound of my feet;
dance to conceal
the pistol under my apron.

#2 (*from the 1950's*)

harriet tubman you are so
black
you make my mother
cry

go from door to northern
door   black is black your
sin is deeper

127

than the dust
in your throat

your skin
is a dark place
you live in

In Mr. Turner's Fields

SAM CORNISH

property of Benjamin
Turner   i still learned
to read
beside my plow in prayer
i prayed and i waited

blacks have always trusted
me for i have always waited
for a sign

i heard a loud move
in the heavens
the serpent was loose
Christ has lain down the yoke

Banneker

RITA DOVE

What did he do except lie
under a pear tree, wrapped in
a great cloak, and meditate
on the heavenly bodies?
Venerable, the good people of Baltimore
whispered, shocked and more than
a little afraid. After all it was said
he took to strong drink.
Why else would he stay out
under the stars all night
and why hadn't he married?

But who would want him! Neither
Ethiopian nor English, neither
lucky nor crazy, a capacious bird
humming as he penned in his mind
another enflamed letter
to President Jefferson—he imagined
the reply, polite and rhetorical.
Those who had been to Philadelphia
reported the statue
of Benjamin Franklin
before the library

his very size and likeness.
A wife? No, thank you.
At dawn he milked
the cows, then went inside
and put on a pot to stew
while he slept. The clock
he whittled as a boy
still ran. Neighbors
woke him up

with warm bread and quilts.
At nightfall he took out

his rifle—a white-maned
figure stalking the darkened
breast of the Union—and
shot at the stars, and by chance
one went out. Had he killed?
I assure thee, my dear Sir!
Lowering his eyes to fields
sweet with the rot of spring, he could see
a government's domed city
rising from the morass and spreading
in a spiral of lights. . . .

David Walker (1785–1830)

Rita Dove

Free to travel, he still couldn't be shown how lucky
he was: *They strip and beat and drag us about*
like rattlesnakes. Home on Brattle Street, he took in the sign
on the door of the slop shop. All day at the counter—
white caps, ale-stained pea coats. Compass: needles,
eloquent as tuning forks, shivered, pointing north.
Evenings, the ceiling fan sputtered like a second pulse.
Oh Heaven! I am full!! I can hardly move my pen!!!

On the faith of an eve-wink, pamphlets were stuffed
into trouser pockets. Pamphlets transported
in the coat linings of itinerant seamen, jackets
ringwormed with salt traded drunkenly to pursers
in the Carolinas, pamphlets ripped out, read aloud:
Men of colour, who are also of sense.
Outrage. Incredulity. Uproar in state legislatures.

We are the most wretched, degraded and abject set
of beings that ever lived since the world began.
The jewelled canaries in the lecture halls tittered,
pressed his dark hand between their gloves.
Every half-step was no step at all.
Every morning, the man on the corner strung a fresh
bunch of boots from his shoulders. "I'm happy!" he said.
"I never want to live any better or happier than
when I can get a-plenty of boots and shoes to clean!"

A second edition. A third.
The abolitionist press is *perfectly appalled.*
Humanity, kindness and the fear of the Lord
does not consist in protecting devils. A month—
his person (is that all?) found face-down
in the doorway at Brattle Street,
his frame slighter than friends remembered.

Saba

Henry Dumas

we weep that our heroes have died
in our memories
our historians and preachers
remind us that we had warriors
who fought the boot of the devils
who came in Jesus ships from Europe

we weep that our forefathers kneeled
and let the knife take our tongues

we weep that no one weeps for us
what is this?
are we what we are?
listen! we are not what we will be
what is this weeping and screaming?

a people cannot create the real hero
until they create the real hero
not by mirrors or masks or muscles
but by men the soil is nourished
and one day
we will not weep but sing him
up

Frederick Douglass

Robert Hayden

When it is finally ours, this freedom, this liberty, this beautiful
and terrible thing, needful to man as air,
usable as earth; when it belongs at last to our children,
when it is truly instinct, brain matter, diastole, systole,
reflex action; when it is finally won; when it is more
than the gaudy mumbo jumbo of politicians:
this man, this Douglass, this former slave, this Negro
beaten to his knees, exiled, visioning a world
where none is lonely, none hunted, alien,
this man, superb in love and logic, this man
shall be remembered. Oh, not with statues' rhetoric,
not with legends and poems and wreaths of bronze alone,
but with the lives grown out of his life, the lives
fleshing his dream of the beautiful, needful thing.

Fired Up!!

for Judy Rollins

EVERETT HOAGLAND

Winnie Mandela got fired from the revolution
today. Her husband fired her over
charges of bribe-taking,
insubordination, charges of insulting
The Queen of England,
whose tourist photo palace was never
bombed,
whose tutored children's grown up matinee,
soap opera lives were never
threatened,
whose womanhood, whose humanity was never
violated, who was never strapped and
tortured
to stay
awake for a week
by electric shock,
charged by static hate, conducted by her own
urine, who never had to take stock of guns,
take charge of a national revolt, a struggle of millions,
and stay beautiful,
giving, giving, giving
her smiling, radiant, defiant persona to a revolution
for a quarter of a century. The Queen

who never raised her own children or genteel, white-gloved
fist in the face of an automatic
weapons-wielding police charge,
without the presence of princely husbanding.

Amandla! The Queen

who never mothered her people
with the blood and blue milk
of a national labor, birth, and afterbirth.
Winnie Mandela, who, while pregnant
with a new nation, lullabyed the fetus with:
We're fired up!
Won't take it any more!!!
We're fired up!
Won't take it any more!!!!

But the government is formed.

Our old, noble, prize-winning Warrior Prince
had high tea with the Queen, who later left for London
and a crown made of melted Krugerrands,
the petrified tears of warrior/women/workers,
the jeweled sweat beads of his nation's minors.

Winnie Mandela was
fired from
the revolution today for rebelliousness,
impropriety, for influence-
peddling, causing embarrassment,
for doing what
she had been asked, told, inspired to do—
for a quarter of a century.

The Old Mongoose—*for Mac*

MURRAY JACKSON

Archwald Lee Wright, born age three,
bobweaved himself into Archie Moore,
roamed the backsides of Union Street
where guards watched for ride robbers.

Stole streetcar change in order to eat,
did time in reform school. Learned
to protect himself with his hands
so he wouldn't have to be reformed.

Archie knew early, before his first fight
with Piano Mover Jones, that it would take
more than taut skin over angry muscle
to punch holes in the heavy bag.

He moved with flashes of light, throwing
hooks and jabs that jarred eardrums.
Always thinking, he finessed opponents.

Outdoors, he forced them to face the sun,
stepped on their toes to keep them from moving.
Stared Carl "Bobo" Olson down in three.

Archie laughed. With his magic diet—
grapefruit, sauerkraut juice and beef:
chew the beef, suck the juice, spit out
the rest—he outlived eight managers.

For Beautiful Mary Brown:
Chicago Rent Strike Leader

June Jordan

All of them are six
who wait inside that other room
where no man walks but many
talk about the many wars

Your baby holds your laboring arms
that bloat from pulling
up and down the stairs to tell
to call the neighbors: We can fight.

She listens to you and she sees
you crying on your knees or else
the dust drifts from your tongue and almost
she can feel her father standing tall.

Came to Chicago like flies to fish.
Found no heroes on the corner.
Butter the bread and cover the couch.
Save on money.

       Don't
tell me how you wash hope hurt and lose
don't tell me how you
sit still at the windowsill:

you will be god to bless you
Mary Brown.

For Etheridge Knight

Lamont B. Steptoe

Hoodoo numberman
empty pockets
filled with the currency
of cell door nights
Heart
a mudswollen river
pregnant with catfish dinners
screamin' neckbone jazz
Preacher
spoutin' cussin' angels
beatin' a tambourine
all the way to the sun

For Malcolm X

MARGARET WALKER

All you violated ones with gentle hearts;
You violent dreamers whose cries shout heartbreak;
Whose voices echo clamors of our cool capers,
And whose black faces have hollowed pits for eyes.
All you gambling sons and hooked children and bowery
      bums
Hating white devils and black bourgeoisie,
Thumbing your noses at your burning red suns,
Gather round this coffin and mourn your dying swan.

Snow-white moslem head-dress around a dead black face!
Beautiful were your sand-papering words against our skins!
Our blood and water pour from your flowing wounds.
You have cut open our breasts and dug scalpels in our
      brains.
When and Where will another come to take your holy place?
Old man mumbling in his dotage, or crying child, unborn?

For Mary McLeod Bethune

MARGARET WALKER

Great Amazon of God behold your bread
washed home again from many distant seas.
The cup of life you lift contains no less,
no bitterness to mock you. In its stead
this sparkling chalice many souls has fed,
and broken hearted people on their knees
lift up their eyes and suddenly they seize
on living faith, and they are comforted.

Believing in the people who are free,
who walk uplifted in an honest way,
you look at last upon another day
that you have fought with God and men to see.
Great Amazon of God behold your bread.
We walk with you and we are comforted.

A Dance for Ma Rainey

AL YOUNG

I'm going to be just like you, Ma
Rainey this monday morning
clouds puffing up out of my head
like those balloons
that float above the faces of white people
in the funny papers

I'm going to hover in the corners
of the world, Ma
& sing from the bottom of hell
up to the tops of high heaven
& send out scratchless waves of yellow
& brown & that basic black honey
misery

I'm going to cry so sweet
& so low
& so dangerous,
Ma,
that the message is going to reach you
back in 1922
where you shimmer
snaggle-toothed
perfumed &
powdered
in your bauble beads
hair pressed & tied back
throbbing with that sick pain
I know
& hide so well
that pain that blues
jives the world with
aching to be heard

that downness
that bottomlessness
first felt by some stolen delta nigger
swamped under with redblooded american agony;
reduced to the sheer shit
of existence
that bred
& battered us all,
Ma,
the beautiful people
our beautiful brave black people
who no longer need to jazz
or sing to themselves in murderous vibrations
or play the veins of their strong tender arms
with needles
to prove that we're still here

7.

A ROCK AGAINST THE WIND

So Long

JAYNE CORTEZ

My man loved me so much
he wanted to kill me
cause he loved me so good
he wanted to die
cause he loved me without sorrow
so sad without tears
he loved me to kill to die to cry
so much he wanted to scream
cause i loved him too much i
drank his tears
loved him too much
i ate his strength
loved him too much i stole his joy
i loved him to drink to eat to steal
cause we loved so much
so good to love to love
so long to love
so long

If I Were Earth

Henry Dumas

Each tear that fell
from the crushed
moons of your face,
stabbed me,
broke and split
into a thousand pains.
But I held out my arms,
and not one did I miss,
no, not one pain.
And if I don't let
you soak into me
and bring me up,
if I don't let you seep
deep into me
and teach me,
then you can cry in
the morning to the sun,
and tell him to rise up
and burn me away.

Seduction

CORNELIUS EADY

I am never alone in this world.
Here are the famous silhouettes on the window shade
And the reason they embrace:

The romantic ballad on the record player
That spills out of the window
Cracked a third of the way open

And down the block, where everyone else is dreaming or trying to
    dream,
Off the walls of the Baptist church,
Off the man who leans on the pharmacy at the corner waiting for the
    phone to ring,
Off the empty seats of the ice-cream parlor,

Around the corner to the all-night grocery
Where the kid behind the bullet-proof glass sways his hips,
His feet making tiny, absent steps upon the floorboards.

It is a spring night, and perhaps every street is like this,
The air rich and edible as fruit.
A couple, returning from a dance,
Takes the center of the sidewalk with a generous, uneven gait,
Aiming for each other's lips, but hitting the eyebrows, the
    forehead . . .

It doesn't matter. Tonight, as I watch from above
We all fall in love,
As would anyone who crosses the lovers' path
As their shadows glide across the front porches,
Brushing against the stoops,
Too busy to notice they're locked in the beat
Or that a light goes out above their heads.

The Anti-Semanticist

EVERETT HOAGLAND

honeystain . . .
the rhetoricians of blackness
matter me not
we are black
and you are beautiful

it matters me not whether
your breasts are american pumpkins or
african gourds
they are full and you are beautiful

it matters me not be your belly
black or brown
it is soft and you are beautiful

it matters me not be your buttocks
bourgeoise or "grass roots"
they are good
and you are beautiful

it matters me not if your bread loaf
thighs
are negro or afro-american
they are round and so ripe
and you are so beautiful

it matters not whether it is
Victoria Falls within your orgasms
instead of Niagara

there is little definition i need
indeed
it matters only that there is

black power
in your loving

this i know
you are beautiful
you are beautiful beyond reference
you are the night interpreted
you are
you

Desire

LANGSTON HUGHES

Desire to us
Was like a double death,
Swift dying
Of our mingled breath,
Evaporation
Of an unknown strange perfume
Between us quickly
In a naked
Room.

Echo

AUDRE LORDE

I hear myself
drought caught   pleading
a windy cause
dry as the earth without rain
crying love
in a tongue of false thunder
while my love waits
a seeded trap
in the door of my house
a mouth full of perfect teeth
sure of their strength upon bone
waits
to swallow me whole
and pass me
as echoes of shadowless laughter.

Quiet   love hangs
in the door of my house
a sheet of brick-caught silk
rent in the sun.

Woman with Flower

Naomi Long Madgett

I wouldn't coax the plant if I were you.
Such watchful nurturing may do it harm.
Let the soil rest from so much digging
And wait until it's dry before you water it.
The leaf's inclined to find its own direction;
Give it a chance to seek the sunlight for itself.

Much growth is stunted by too careful prodding,
Too eager tenderness.
The things we love we have to learn to leave alone.

She Is Flat On Her Back

(for K. F.)

E. ETHELBERT MILLER

she is flat on her back
when she decides / she decides
it's time to make that move
she rises from the bed
she says

   i'll be right back
   i'm not protected

and it is at that time / now
i wonder about the danger that i am
the terrible thing i must be
that she needs to be protected
and it is not the fear of children
the fear of having children
it is me
that she fears / i think

as i lie in the dark
staring at the ceiling
listening to her move around
in the bathroom
the opening of closets
the sound of water
the turning on / and off of lights

and now
she is back
next to me
her hand back in place
where she left me

and i am vulnerable
to love
i am not protected
i am vulnerable to love
   to love

Omnivore

HARRYETTE MULLEN

Because I was afraid to lose you
I swallowed stones
chewed metal
sucked bullets through my teeth

While you licked sugar
I pocketed salt
I burned my tears
cooked my blues
and ate the smoke

And still you left me
spilling all my hungers
my belly split open
full of wonders
like an ancient fish

The Joy

HARRYETTE MULLEN

Here's a bowl of batter
for your spoon to stir.
Here's an oven
to bake your bread in.
Put some starch
in your chef's hat, honey,
and start cookin.

Pretty Piece of Tail

Harryette Mullen

Pretty piece of tail,
now I wanted you so bad.
Nice, pretty piece of tail
and I wanted it mighty bad.
I thought if I could get it,
that piece be the best I ever had.

She had her legs together
the way her mama said she should.
Yeah, she was keeping her legs together
just like her mama say she should.
The way she was holding on to it,
I knew it must be good.

I schemed and lied to get it,
told her I loved her best.
That's right, I schemed and I lied to get it,
told the girl I loved her best.
Soon as I tried that little bit of tail,
I knew it was no better than the rest.

When I first saw you, baby,
I told you I'd love you until I die.
First time I saw you, looking so good now, baby,
said I'd love you till I die.
Well now I'll tell you, if you didn't know, darling,
a man's just born to lie.

That's the truth, I'll testify.

If I was on the jury,
talking about courts and jail—
If I was on the jury
wouldn't no man go to jail
just for trying out a pretty piece of tail.

(For Poki)

A. X. NICHOLAS

1.

Strange
      that we wake
in the center of the night/
      the naked image-of-ourselves
locked black & beautifully together on this bed.

2.

The sand & miles-of-water
before us/
      our Black bodies
blending with this night/
      the far city
floating (How strange!) in this sky.

3.

Strange
      how your thighs
tremble like the tomtom-of-drums in the night/
      opening/closing
hot & dark as Africa round my waist.

Levitation

CARL PHILLIPS

While presumably you
are flying over fields of wild mustard,
deliberate blues and sandstone
that are flax and everything else
flax isn't,

I have spent the days without you
naked and dreaming the traffic
from our bed. The sheets play
Eastern, the right
buttock and elbow rub up against
thin Chinese and blue, outsized
flowers that cannot exist, but
unwind around
and under the body that is always
mine to forget about.

I watch the light in tight cubes raise itself
to powers of brightness
commanding all eyes shut,
and feel the sheets go cinnamon
at my heel (fretting truant, the last to rise),

then wait for the conquering dream
to come, in which the phone
rings, and knowing
it can only be you, I pass
away from it, into the living room,
my frame shifting over the magazines, litter
of old cups, plates,
and printing the teak-dark floor
with shadow, my body
the one lost cloud.

Imagine my flesh
(leaves waiting to unfurl
in blue sheets)

conquering the dream of you,
as the rooms of my life with you
spin to miniatures below me: the pear
you didn't finish, your votive shoes,
bits I am even now forgetting.

Highflown: Love

EUGENE B. REDMOND

In the highflown language
Of moon travelers
Social scientists sort our hurts—
Add their smog-crippled vision—
And rearranged our private pains
Along the Wall Street of current demands;
And my people become the
Cocaine that makes America high:
Become dreams
America sucks through maniacal straws of sleep;
Discounting our lore,
The scientists say we *cannot love*
               say our needs are numbed:
But sometimes,
When you construct knots in my throat
And your lips re-create my heartclock,
I am hypnotized by the aggregate passion
Of my past   by the sum of my historical ecstasy:
A power we know
Cannot be stilled by airborne theories of scholars
Nestled in Freudian citadels:
A power that cannot be seen
Heard
Or flattened to fit the pages of a book.

—answer to yo / question
of am i not yo / woman
even if u went on shit again—

SONIA SANCHEZ

& i a beginner
                in yo / love
say no.
                i wud not be yo / woman
& see u disappear
                        each day
befo my eyes
                and know yo /
reappearance
                to be
                        a one /
                                nite / stand.
no man.
                blk/
                lovers   cannot   live
in wite powder that removes
them from they blk/selves
                                cannot ride
majestic / wite / horses
                                in a machine age.
blk / lovers
                must live /
                        push against the
devils of this world
                        against the creeping
witeness of they own minds.
I am yo / woman
                my man.
                                and blk/women
deal in babies and
                sweet / blk / kisses
and nites that
                multiply by twos.

The Source of the Singing

MARILYN NELSON WANIEK

Under everything, everything
a movement, slow as hair growth,
as the subtle click of cells turning
into other cells, the life in us
that grows as mountains grow.
Under everything this movement,
stars and wind circle around the smaller
circles of the grass, and the birds caged
in the kitchen sing it over and over,
inexplicably in their sweet chirps.

I feel it like sometimes like today
somewhere in my torso, perhaps
sweet in the belly; this must be
what carrying a child is like.
I sit at a table and feel something
move with the pain of just before tears.
What is it the body says to me,
these tender aches that make me glad?
Not even one syllable is clear,
but if you were near I would tell you,
and you might lay your hand where the talking
starts and the pain, where my life
is still moving like an eaten live thing
and push your warmth into mine,
here, into the source of the singing.

8.

IS SHE OUR SISTER?

Whispers in a Country Church

ALVIN AUBERT

Who's that dark woman
Sittin' next to the preacher
Eyeing his feet?
Lord, look at her.
Red hat.
Flowers.
Perfume you can smell
From here.
Look. Making a move.
Asking for water.
Clumsy thing—
All over his
Brand new shoes.
Just what she wanted.
Bending down that way,
Wonder that dress don't split.
Pretty hair, though.
Got to give her that.

The Mother

GWENDOLYN BROOKS

Abortions will not let you forget.
You remember the children you got that you did not get,
The damp small pulps with a little or with no hair,
The singers and workers that never handled the air.
You will never neglect or beat
Them, or silence or buy with a sweet.
You will never wind up the sucking-thumb
Or scuttle off ghosts that come.
You will never leave them, controlling your luscious sigh,
Return for a snack of them, with gobbling mother-eye.

I have heard in the voices of the wind the voices of my
         dim killed children.
I have contracted. I have eased
My dim dears at the breasts they could never suck.
I have said, Sweets, if I sinned, if I seized
Your luck
And your lives from your unfinished reach,
If I stole your births and your names,
Your straight baby tears and your games,
Your stilted or lovely loves, your tumults, your marriages,
         aches, and your deaths,
If I poisoned the beginnings of your breaths,
Believe that even in my deliberateness I was not deliberate.
Though why should I whine,
Whine that the crime was other than mine?—
Since anyhow you are dead.
Or rather, or instead,
You were never made.
But that too, I am afraid,
Is faulty: oh, what shall I say, how is the truth to be said?
You were born, you had body, you died.
It is just that you never giggled or planned or cried.

Believe me, I loved you all.
Believe me, I knew you, though faintly, and I loved, I loved you
All.

Jessie Mitchell's Mother

GWENDOLYN BROOKS

Into her mother's bedroom to wash the ballooning body.
"My mother is jelly-hearted and she has a brain of jelly:
Sweet, quiver-soft, irrelevant. Not essential.
Only a habit would cry if she should die.
A pleasant sort of fool without the least iron. . . .
Are you better, mother, do you think it will come today?"
The stretched yellow rag that was Jessie Mitchell's mother
Reviewed her. Young, and so thin, and so straight.
So straight! as if nothing could ever bend her.
But poor men would bend her, and doing things with poor men,
Being much in bed, and babies would bend her over,
And the rest of things in life that were for poor women,
Coming to them grinning and pretty with intent to bend and to kill.
Comparisons shattered her heart, ate at her bulwarks:
The shabby and the bright: she, almost hating her daughter,
Crept into an old sly refuge: "Jessie's black
And her way will be black, and jerkier even than mine.
Mine, in fact, because I was lovely, had flowers
Tucked in the jerks, flowers were here and there. . . ."
She revived for the moment settled and dried-up triumphs,
Forced perfume into old petals, pulled up the droop,
Refueled
Triumphant long-exhaled breaths.
Her exquisite yellow youth. . . .

Virginia Portrait

STERLING A. BROWN

Winter is settling on the place; the sedge
Is dry and lifeless and the woods stand bare.
The late autumnal flowers, nipped by frost,
Break from the sear stalks in the trim, neat garden,
And fall unheeded on the bleak, brown earth.

The winter of her year has come to her,
This wizened woman, spare of frame, but great
Of heart, erect, and undefeated yet.

Grief has been hers, before this wintry time.
Death has paid calls, unmannered, uninvited;
Low mounds have swollen in the fenced off corner,
Over brown children, marked by white-washed stones.
She has seen hopes that promised a fine harvest
Burnt by the drought; or bitten by the hoarfrost;
Or washed up and drowned out by unlooked for rains.
And as a warning blast of her own winter,
Death, the harsh overseer, shouted to her man,
Who answering slowly went over the hill.

She, puffing on a jagged slow-burning pipe,
By the low hearthfire, knows her winter now.
But she has strength and steadfast hardihood.
Deep-rooted is she, even as the oaks,
Hardy as perennials about her door.
The circle of the seasons brings no fear,
"Folks all gits used to what dey sees so often";
And she has helps that throng her glowing fire
Mixed with the smoke hugging her grizzled head:

Warm friends, the love of her full-blooded spouse,
Quiet companionship as age crept on him,

Laughter of babies, and their shrewd, sane raising;
These simple joys, not poor to her at all;
The sight of smokeclouds pouring from the flue;
Her stalwart son deep busied with "book larnin',"
After the weary fields; the kettle's purr
In duet with the sleek and pampered mouser;
Twanging of dominickers; lowing of Betsey;
Old folksongs chanted underneath the stars. . . .

Even when winter settles on her heart,
She keeps a wonted, quiet nonchalance,
A courtly dignity of speech and carriage,
Unlooked for in these distant rural ways.
She has found faith sufficient for her grief,
The song of earth for bearing heavy years,
She with slow speech, and spurts of heartfelt laughter,
Illiterate, and somehow very wise.

She has been happy, and her heart is grateful.
Now she looks out, and forecasts unperturbed
Her following slowly over the lonesome hill,
Her *'layin' down her burdens, bye and bye.'*

the lost baby poem

LUCILLE CLIFTON

the time i dropped your almost body down
down to meet the waters under the city
and run one with the sewage to the sea
what did i know about waters rushing back
what did i know about drowning
or being drowned

you would have been born into winter
in the year of the disconnected gas
and no car   we would have made the thin
walk over genesee hill into the canada wind
to watch you slip like ice into strangers' hands
you would have fallen naked as snow into winter
if you were here i could tell you these
and some other things

if i am ever less than a mountain
for your definite brothers and sisters
let the rivers pour over my head
let the sea take me for a spiller
of seas   let black men call me stranger
always   for your never named sake

later i'll say
i spent my life
loving a great man

later
my life will accuse me
of various treasons

not black enough
too black

eyes closed when they should have been open
eyes open when they should have been closed

will accuse me for unborn babies
and dead trees

later
when i defend again and again
with this love
my life will keep silent
listening to
my body breaking

song at midnight

LUCILLE CLIFTON

brothers,
this big woman
carries much sweetness
in the folds of her flesh.
her hair
is white with wonderful.
she is
rounder than the moon
and far more faithful.
brothers,
who will hold her,
who will find her beautiful
if you do not?

won't you celebrate with me
what i have shaped into
a kind of life? i had no model.
born in babylon
both nonwhite and woman
what did i see to be except myself?
i made it up
here on this bridge between
starshine and clay,
my one hand holding tight
my other hand; come celebrate
with me that everyday
something has tried to kill me
and has failed.

Grinding Vibrato

JAYNE CORTEZ

Blues Lady
with the beaded face
painted lips
and hair smeared
in the oil of texas

You were looking good and sounding beautiful
until the horseman wanted your thunder
until the boa constrictor wanted your body
until syringes upright hyenas
barbwired your meat to their teeth
pushing behind your ears
inside your mouth
between your vagina
scabs the size of quarters
scabs the size of pennies
the size of the shape of you
all pigeon holes and spider legs colonized woman
funky piece of blood flint
with blue graffitied arms
a throat of dead bees
and swollen fingers that dig into a swamp of broken purrtongue

Spotted stripped blues lady
who was looking good and sounding beautiful
with those nasal love songs
those strident battle-cry songs
that copper maroon rattle resonator
shaking from your feet to your eyes
the sound of water drum songs
grinding vibrato songs to work by to make love by
to remember you by

Blues song lady who was looking good and sounding beautiful
until you gave away your thunder
until you gave up your spirit
until you barbwired your meat to teeth
and became the odor of hyenas
uprooted woman with the embalmed face
pall bearer lips
and hair matted in the mud of texas
how many ounces of revolution do you need
to fill the holes in your body
or
is it too late to get back your lightning
is it too late to reconstruct your song blues song sister tell me
is it too late for the mother tongue in your womanself to insurrect

On the Turning Up of Unidentified Black Female Corpses

Toi Derricotte

Mowing his three acres with a tractor,
a man notices something ahead—a mannequin—
he thinks someone threw it from a car. Closer
he sees it is the body of a black woman.

The medics come and turn her with pitchforks.
Her gaze shoots past him to nothing. Nothing
is explained. How many black women
have been turned up to stare at us blankly,

in weedy fields, off highways,
pushed out in plastic bags,
shot, knifed, unclothed partially, raped,
their wounds sealed with a powdery crust.

Last week on TV, a gruesome face, eyes bloated shut.
No one will say, "She looks like she's sleeping," ropes
of blue-black slashes at the mouth. Does anybody
know this woman? Will anyone come forth? Silence

like a backwave rushes into that field
where, just the week before, four other black girls
had been found. The gritty image hangs in the air
just a few seconds, but it strikes me,

a black woman, there is a question being asked
about my life. How can I
protect myself? Even if I lock my doors,
walk only in the light, someone wants me dead.

Am I wrong to think
if five white women had been stripped,

broken, the sirens would wail until
someone was named?

Is it any wonder I walk over these bodies
pretending they are not mine, that I do not know
the killer, that I am just like any woman—
if not wanted, at least tolerated.

Part of me wants to disappear, to pull
the earth on top of me. Then there is this part
that digs me up with this pen
and turns my sad black face to the light.

Canary

for Michael S. Harper

RITA DOVE

Billie Holiday's burned voice
had as many shadows as lights,
a mournful candelabra against a sleek piano,
the gardenia her signature under that ruined face.

(Now you're cooking, drummer to bass,
magic spoon, magic needle.
Take all day if you have to
with your mirror and your bracelet of song.)

Fact is, the invention of women under siege
has been to sharpen love in the service of myth.

If you can't be free, be a mystery.

. . . And the Old Women Gathered

(The Gospel Singers)

MARI EVANS

and the old women gathered
and sang His praises
standing
resolutely together
like supply sergeants who
have seen
everything
and are still
Regular Army: It
was fierce and
not melodic and
although we ran
the sound of it
stayed in our ears . . .

Black Queen Blues

(Finale)

MARI EVANS

Heyyy mama . . .
    Whuts
  to it
  Sistuhh . . . ?

Manchild floatin on y'hip
    girlchile
pullin on y'skirttail
  The songs say
     you are a Black

    Queen

  Say you "three times
a Lady . . ."

   Why arent you
    dancing
   to the music

She

for Carolyn Grace

CHRISTOPHER GILBERT

When she sits at the kitchen table
while she talks her hands seem to balance
in the air faithful at the level of
her words; she is careful what she says.
The morning sun through the window strikes
her skin, shows how the faint lines in her
palms will come to deepen like corduroy
cloth to fit the weather of her age.
Still a young woman, she has to work
the graveyard shift, sleeps what is left,
then wakes to get the kids to school.
It must be morning when she dreams.
Peering into her coffee's surface
she looks back from its depth, her hands
caught holding an implement, a fossil of
her life: Alabama born, feelings
huddled north, these steel cities this cold month,
her dark soul twisting into fingers
whose motion at this brown angle
is the slow fall flight of leaves through time.
And she rises with the gesture, and
the oil in her hands is necessity's
sweat: each hand on the tabletop
a work cloth rubbing the other fine
wooden one.

Soft Targets

for Black Girls

ESSEX HEMPHILL

He was arrested and detained
for nailing Barbie doll heads
to telephone poles.

He was beaten
while in custody, accused.

After healing, he resumed
his irreverent campaign,
this outlawed spook terrorist
continued hammering horse nails

through Barbie heads
and setting them aflame.

Barbie never told Black girls
they are beautiful.

She never acknowledged
their breathtaking Negritude.

She never told them
to possess their own souls.

They were merely shadows
clutching the edges of her mirror.

Barbie never told Black girls
they are beautiful,

not in the ghetto evenings
after double dutch,

nor in the integrated suburbs,
after ballet class.

Stations

AUDRE LORDE

Some women love
to wait
for life   for a ring
in the June light   for a touch
of the sun to heal them   for another
woman's voice   to make them whole
to untie their hands
put words in their mouths
form to their passages   sound
to their screams   for some other sleeper
to remember   their future   their past.

Some women wait for their right
train   in the wrong station
in the alleys of morning
for the noon to holler
the night come down.

Some women wait for love
to rise up
the child of their promise
to gather from earth
what they do not plant
to claim pain for labor
to become
the tip of an arrow   to aim
at the heart of now
but it never stays.

Some women wait for visions
that do not return
where they were not welcome
naked

for invitations to places
they always wanted
to visit
to be repeated.

Some women wait for themselves
around the next corner
and call the empty spot peace
but the opposite of living
is only not living
and the stars do not care.

Some women wait for something
to change   and nothing
does change
so they change
themselves.

The Old Women

NAOMI LONG MADGETT

They are young.
They do not understand
what the old women are saying.

They see the gnarled hands raised
and think they are praying.
They cannot see the weapons hung

between their fingers. When the mouths
gape and the rasping noises
crunch like dead leaves,

they laugh at the voices
they think are trying to sing.
They are young

and have not learned
the many faces of endurance, the furtive
triumphs earned through suffering.

1915 Interior

CLARENCE MAJOR

sister, you open
like a beautiful wide fan.
you must be the opening
to the greatest secret, the
truth: the ancient riddle.
sister, how you spread
and your center is
never revealed, how you
grow wider and smoother
and your depth is
unending, opening with-
out pressure lightly.
giving light, giving
me myself

Illusion

COLLEEN J. McELROY

I hate wide mouth black girls
with their loud walnut faces.
I hate their bright white eyes
and evil tongues,

their hen cackle laughs
that startle birds
roosting in trees miles away.
I hate their graceful jungle steps,
the steps they fall into too easily,
a downbeat only they can hear.

They stir cities,
cause concrete to tremble.
I hate the way their backs
taper into a narrow base
before spreading, graceful
round and proud as a peacock's.

Their firm black legs
insult me with swift movements,
feet in tempo even as they walk
to pick up the evening paper;
turning pages noisily to find
comic strips, the rustle of paper
paced with the pop of many sticks
of Juicy Fruit.

I hate the popping fingers,
the soft flash of color
turning like butterscotch buds
in a field of wind wild
dandelion greens.

I turn away from high cheek bones
and wide spread mocha nostrils
finely honed to catch the scent
of paddy-rollers or pig faced sheriffs.

This country has made them
sassyfaced.
They sneer at mousey mongoloid blondes
who move coolly blind
through a forest of suburbs,
lisping about posh uptown hotels.

I hate the pain that makes them
bulldog their way through
downtown crowds,
makes them nurture dead minds
and naturally accent cheap clothes
with finely curved licorice colored shoulders.

They bury Nefertiti charms
under outstretched lips,
grow older under frowns
and a hurricane of bad manners;

they grow barbed, cold,
these Sapphires and Mabel Sues
from ebony to dusky brown,
from creme and rust to lemon yellow.

They are my sisters
and we sit in a barracks of noise,
trading screams with wandering
no-caring   louder   brothers.

The Circus of the City

Colleen J. McElroy

Crazy Mary dreams the city while she's awake
She lets us watch, her hands orchestrating
Traffic like a blind conductor at a mad concert
She's crazy, we know that, yet we always
Inspect the air in case she isn't faking

When she bumps and grinds her pelvis against a clean-
Cut young man's zipper and teases, *Want it, dearie?*
We see the world in a glance and Crazy Mary performing
Dreams while the city dreams itself awake

    In city center, a thing is wrapped in rags and rides a bicycle
    The thing is silent and obedient and smells of burning dust
    The thing is wrapped in ace bandages, gray and unchanging
    In Kansas City, a thing walked on his hands and sang arias
    New York crazies have unions; in Summersville they marry
    Each city is allowed to worry at least one crazy into existence

When I was young, home was black folks who never thought to fit
Other folks believed our streets were filled with crazies
Now streets hold things and businessmen benign with malignant
Interest rates, and women insistently becoming
Something else depending on the season
I don't want to be them

Corners are crowded with legions of good-cause workers
Visionaries and wall-eyed beggars who whisper for pennies
Cracks of buildings are stuffed with birds tie-dyed with soot
I don't want to be them

    Crazy Mary says this place, pure and simple
    Was built for piemen and jugglers
    She keeps defining eternity, telling us we're in it

All the while stashing clouds in her shopping bags
And when she looks up, we expect rain

Did you know the sky is falling, dear? she asks
How the Hell should I know, I answer
I didn't know Humpty Dumpty was an egg until
I was fifteen and by then, all knowing was too late
Crazy Mary laughs and vanishes into traffic

I want to be the woman who levitates on her own terms
Who falls asleep under the magician's thumbs
Who believes air is no longer invisible
Who will sing at top lung in public places
Who listens to deep-voiced commands to go away
And won't

Crazy Mary beats the air into obedience
Crazy Mary dreams getting out and won't give up
Her life is a scarf pulled from a hollow tube
A bunny from an empty hat

I watch that trick she does with words
The way no matter where she starts
They all come out right
I let her teach me to say
Take me with you Mary; take me with you

Lessons from a Mirror

Thylias Moss

Snow White was nude at her wedding, she's so white
the gown seemed to disappear when she put it on.

Put me beside her and the proximity is good
for a study of chiaroscuro, not much else.

Her name aggravates me most, as if I need to be told
what's white and what isn't.

Judging strictly by appearance there's a future for me
forever at her heels, a shadow's constant worship.

Is it fair for me to live that way, unable
to get off the ground?

Turning the tables isn't fair unless they keep turning.
Then there's the danger of Russian roulette

and my disadvantage: nothing falls from the sky
to name me.

I am the empty space where the tooth was, that my tongue
rushes to fill because I can't stand vacancies.

And it's not enough. The penis just fills another
gap. And it's not enough.

When you look at me,
know that more than white is missing.

Anatomy

HARRYETTE MULLEN

1. The Ovaries
Easter baskets,
matching egg cups of the flesh,
twin satellites of the moon.

Hot and cold faucets
turning on alternate months.

Maracas shaking their seeds
to the rhythm of blood.

A pair of bulbs
planted in body's earth
bloom to flowers
blossoming blood.

2. The Tubes
Perfect roads,
or snakes; ribbons
to tie into knots.

Jam up the tunnel
hope it won't explode.

3. The Womb
The warmest garment,
it grows like skin.
The most comfortable room,
it contains no furniture.
The easiest house,
it builds itself.
The most generous country,
where the climate's always good.

Let the world go into
its womb again.
Turn out the lights,
enjoy the dark.

4. The Breasts

They are food
that likes to be eaten.

5. The Vagina

Tear this envelope open
gently for the letter inside
addressed to you,
that you'll read and reread
again and again,
till the red ink fades
into your hands,
till you know it in your veins.

Eyes in the Back of Her Head

Harryette Mullen

I'm your momma, and I could always tell when
you're doin somethin you aint got no business.
Hell, I know you: I birthed you.
Saw you before you saw yourself.
Watched you climb a chair to the
kitchen's highest shelf and steal
a sip of whiskey,
just to know how it felt going down your throat.
You choked, but I beat you for it anyway,
cause the stuff aint made for kids to waste.
'Sides, was too early for you to get to likin that taste.

Yeah, I'm your momma, got eyes in the back of my
          head.
I guessed what you'd do before you did it.
I knew your secret before you thought,
and hid it.
And, hey, you better look down, child,
don't roll your eyes at me.
You can aim those bullets but
you can't shoot em.
I mean, your young eyes aint no
match for mine.
Or for the minefields you got to walk through blind
cause you won't let my old sight
see you through.

Now I want to close
those momma's extra eyes,
since you can't see what they see,
or let them see for you.
Since they won't keep me smug against

the things that hurt me once,
that will hurt me twice.

I'm your momma (she always said).
Yeah, I've got eyes in the back of my head.
Eyes that see where you're goin,
where I've been.

Tune for a Teenage Niece

for Jeanine Spencer

Eugene B. Redmond

Smile/rippling river of dance—
Flow, blow green soul-lyre
Ballooning under brown flesh:
Song/swirl, startling as claps
Of unexpected waves;
Girlriver dancing its drumdeep past,
Its boogalooborn/e day,
Fluteflown afro freight
*Grand*mother/mamma/aunt—sun-led—
Yesterwhistling confluence
        /childwoman and charmsong:
        "Brown blues and honey-river, girl!
        Blues-brown and river-honey, girl!
        Girlmother gonna sing her song someday, boy!
        Brown blues and honey-river, girl!"
Smile/river dancing, splashing flame-waves
Applaud and burn/mold *brownfruit,*
Afro-plum,
River symphony, water ritual:
        "Brown blues and honey-river, girl!"
Girlriver, spiced as pot liquor, flowing up/under
From queenmother's heartbeam; from magic and marmelade;
Fluteflown to fleshdance and birdgrace:
Flowing to *omen,* to *woman:*
        "Brown blues and honey-river, girl!"

Feminism

CAROLYN RODGERS

our mothers,
when asked
may speak of us
in terms of our accomplishments.
my daughter is a flower
shedding buds of brown babies.
she holds two diplomas in
her fists as she shows her
obliqueness to a world that
only cares for credentials.
what is your claim to fame?
what is your claim to life—
when there are no diplomas
to be lauded,
no husband to be pillared upon,
no buds to be babied.
when does the wind blow on your face
and in what direction do you turn
when it rains?

There is a House

LAMONT B. STEPTOE

There is a house
with all the rooms filled with Momma
but there is a river
that separates me from this house
it is a wide river
a river so wide that
it must be called a sea
yes, a sea
a sea so wide
that it must be called time
yes, time
a time so wide
that it must be called death
yes, death

Old Black Ladies Standing on Bus Stop Corners #2

for my grandmother, Leona Smith

QUINCY TROUPE

blue black & bow bent under, beautiful
blue black & bow bent under, beautiful
blue black & bow bent under, beautiful

& it never did matter
whether the weather
was flame-tongue-licked
or as cold as a welldigger's asshole
in late december when santa claus
was working his cold money bullshit
that made financiers grin ear to ear
all the way to secret bank vaults
overflowing with marble eyes
of dirt-poor children

blue black & bow bent under, beautiful
blue black & bow bent under, beautiful
blue black & bow bent under, beautiful

never did matter
whether the days were storm raked
unzipped by lightning streaking clouds
dropping tornadoes that skipped crazy
to their own exploding beat
shooting hailstone death—
that popped like old bones—
crashing into the skulled
sunken eyes of tired old ladies
tired old black ladies
standing on bus stop corners
pain wrapped as shawls around their necks

blue black & bow bent under, beautiful

& "mama" it didn't matter
that your pained scarred feet overworked
numb legs grew down out of old worn dresses
seemingly fragile, gaunt & skeletal frail
as two old mop sticks—scarecrow legs—
didn't matter because you stood there anyway
defying nature's chameleon weather—
cold as a welldigger's asshole, then oven-hot—
defying all reason, you stood
there, testifying over 300 years
stretching back, of madness & treason

blue black & bow bent under, beautiful

no, it didn't matter
because the beauty of your heroic life
grown lovely in twisted swamps
grown lovely in a loveless land
grown pure & full from wombs
of concrete blood & bones
of concrete blood & bones & death
of death & sweat chained to breath
didn't matter dark proud flower
who stood tall scrubbed by cold
& rain & heat & age carrying
the foreign name given your grandfather—
who swayed body high
twisting & turning in the breeze
like billie's "strange fruit"—

because you stood there anyway
unforgettably silent in your standing
beautiful work-scarred black lady
numb legs & bow bent under beautiful
stood there on pain-scarred feet overworked
numb legs
& bow bent under beautiful
under the memory of your grandfather swaying high
up there in a burning southern breeze

now sweet music love sings soft tender beauty
                              deep in your washed aging windows—
& you give me strength
                              during the mad, bizarre days—

& we have learned to love your life
& will vindicate the pain & silence of your life
the memory of your grandfather with the foreign name
& who sways high up there in history over your legs
                              blue black & bow bent under beautiful
the weight of over 300 years carried
of blood & bones & death in mud
of breath & sweat chained to death
                              numb legs & bow bent under beautiful
under the memory of your grandfather
swaying high up there in the burning breeze

            didn't matter whether the weather was flame-tongue-licked
or as cold as a welldigger's asshole in late december
because you stood there anyway
in full bloom of your strength & rare beauty
& made us strong

blue black & bow bent under, beautiful
blue black & bow bent under, beautiful
blue black & bow bent under, beautiful

Mama I Remember

MARILYN NELSON WANIEK

Mama I remember.
My hair was in braids—
you tapped done with the comb
and I stood up between your knees.
You were always
packing for the movers,
sitting in front of me
when I touched my father's hair.
You never cried,
wrapped glasses in newspaper,
took the pictures down.
The last baby grew
warped in your womb,
smiled three years
and died. I remember
your eyes when you climbed
into the ambulance.
You patted my cheek,
your hands wet with blood.

You stared
when I slapped the wall
and cursed the hospital
where my father died.
Now you meditate.
I understand
your need, the soft ache
of loss in your thighs.

9.

DON'T IT MAKE YOU WANT TO CRY?

Blood to Blood

ALVIN AUBERT

it may be a little different
nowadays but when i was a boy
everyblackoneofus had his own
private lynching.   carried it
'round with him in his front
pocket, close to his private
parts.   blood to blood.

Young Soul

AMIRI BARAKA

First, feel, then feel, then
read, or read, then feel, then
fall, or stand, where you
already are. Think
of your self, and the other
selves . . . think
of your parents, your mothers
and sisters, your bentslick
father, then feel, or
fall, on your knees
if nothing else will move you,

> then read
> and look deeply
> into all matters
> come close to you
> city boys—
> country men
>
> Make some muscle
> in your head, but
> use the muscle
> in yr heart

We Real Cool

GWENDOLYN BROOKS

The Pool Players
Seven at the Golden Shovel.

We real cool. We
Left school. We

Lurk late. We
Strike straight. We

Sing sin. We
Thin gin. We

Jazz June. We
Die soon.

Strong Men

STERLING A. BROWN

They dragged you from homeland,
They chained you in coffles,
They huddled you spoon-fashion in filthy hatches,
They sold you to give a few gentlemen ease.

They broke you in like oxen,
They scourged you,
They branded you,
They made your women breeders,
They swelled your numbers with bastards. . . .
They taught you the religion they disgraced.

You sang:
    Keep a-inchin' along
    Lak a po' inch worm. . . .

You sang:
    Bye and bye
    I'm gonna lay down dis heaby load. . . .

You sang:
    Walk togedder, chillen,
    Dontcha git weary. . . .
        The strong men keep a-comin' on
        The strong men git stronger.

They point with pride to the roads you built for them,
They ride in comfort over the rails you laid for them.
They put hammers in your hands
And said—Drive so much before sundown.

You sang:
    Ain't no hammah

In dis lan',
Strikes lak mine, bebby,
Strikes lak mine.

They cooped you in their kitchens,
They penned you in their factories,
They gave you the jobs that they were too good for,
They tried to guarantee happiness to themselves
By shunting dirt and misery to you.

You sang:
 Me an' muh baby gonna shine, shine
 Me an' muh baby gonna shine.

  The strong men keep a-comin' on
  The strong men git stronger. . . .

They bought off some of your leaders
You stumbled, as blind men will . . .
They coaxed you, unwontedly soft-voiced. . . .
You followed a way.
Then laughed as usual.

They heard the laugh and wondered;
Uncomfortable;
Unadmitting a deeper terror. . . .
  The strong men keep a-comin' on
  Gittin' stronger. . . .

What, from the slums
Where they have hemmed you,
What, from the tiny huts
They could not keep from you—
What reaches them
Making them ill at ease, fearful?
Today they shout prohibition at you
"Thou shalt not this"
"Thou shalt not that"
"Reserved for whites only"
You laugh.

One thing they cannot prohibit—
    The strong men . . . coming on
    The strong men gittin' stronger.
    Strong men. . . .
    Stronger. . . .

those boys that ran together

LUCILLE CLIFTON

those boys that ran together
at Tillman's
and the poolroom
everybody see them now
think it's a shame

everybody see them now
remember they was fine boys

we have some fine black boys

don't it make you want to cry?

Portraiture

ANITA SCOTT COLEMAN

Black men are the tall trees that remain
Standing in a forest after a fire.
 Flames strip their branches,
 Flames sear their limbs,
 Flames scorch their trunks.
 Yet stand these trees
 For their roots are thrust deep
 In the heart of the earth.
Black men are the tall trees that remain
Standing in a forest after a fire.

Knees of a Natural Man

(for Jay Wright)

Henry Dumas

my ole man took me to the fulton fish market
we walk around in the guts and the scales

my ole man show me a dead fish, eyes like throat spit
he say "you hongry boy?" i say "naw, not yet"

my ole man show me how to pick the leavings
he say people throw away fish that not rotten

we scaling on our knees back uptown on lenox
sold five fish, keepin one for the pot

my ole man copped a bottle of wine
he say, "boy, build me a fire out in the lot"

backyard cat climbin up my leg for fish
i make a fire in the ash can

my ole man come when he smell fish
frank williams is with him, they got wine

my ole man say "the boy cotch the big one"
he tell big lie and slap me on the head

i give the guts to the cat and take me some wine
we walk around the sparks like we in hell

my ole man is laughin and coughin up wine
he say "you hongry boy?" i say "naw, not yet"

next time i go to fulton fish market
first thing i do is take a long drink of wine

Gifts

MURRAY JACKSON

I.

I stood in the tunnel warehouse
holding hands with my brother and Dad,
with our Red Flyer wagon that the Goodfellows left.
We came for potatoes, salt pork, beans, and flour.
The lines were long, but we had to stay. Strangers
waited with us, against the flush of winter.

II.

Lunch at the Book Cadillac, second basement.
Our uncle worked in the Kay Danzer Flower Shop.
He took roses to the stadium ticket window.
We got to see the Tigers play the Yankees.
Greenberg hit one out onto Cherry Street.

III.

I had a report due in Social Science.
Finished it while Mom did the dishes.
I washed my safety-patrol belt every Monday.
Mr. Loving expected them to be spotless.
I brushed, scrubbed, and soaked it.
Mom suggested table salt. It glowed.

IV.

Mom told Dad I wanted to go to college.
We didn't have money for school.
Dad pulled out the blue pin-striped suit
that he saved for special good times,
looked it over, fondled the jacket, took the suit
to Lewis's, the pawnshop on Gratiot.

San Diego Goodbye—1944, *Jacksaw Arena*

MURRAY JACKSON

Oxhead McIntosh, out of White Plains,
could hit hard. I was quicker.
He was always talkin', "Nigger boy,
where'd you get those funny green eyes?
You know you ain't supposed to win."

I couldn't keep my mind on the fight.
"Black boy, I'm beatin' your ass."

He dropped his right to hammer me
with his left. I slipped the punch
and landed a left hook to the jaw.
His jaw dropped, splintered, hung
like a door with a missing hinge.

He clutched and fell, whirled
upright, then dropped, pawing his jaw
to push the hurt away.

I stood in the corner, ready
to break his face again. Then
I saw his eyes—panicked, hurt, lost.
Blood trickled from his lips
and splattered the canvas.

I climbed through the ropes for the last time.

Sonnet to a Negro in Harlem

HELENE JOHNSON

You are disdainful and magnificent—
Your perfect body and your pompous gait,
Your dark eyes flashing solemnly with hate;
Small wonder that you are incompetent
To imitate those whom you so despise—
Your shoulders towering high above the throng,
Your head thrown back in rich, barbaric song,
Palm trees and mangoes stretched before your eyes.
Let others toil and sweat for labor's sake
And wring from grasping hands their meed of gold.
Why urge ahead your supercilious feet?
Scorn will efface each footprint that you make.
I love your laughter, arrogant and bold.
You are too splendid for this city street!

Losses

Yusef Komunyakaa

After Nam he lost himself,
   not trusting his hands
      with loved ones.

His girlfriend left,
   & now he scouts the edge of town,
      always with one ear

cocked & ready to retreat,
   to blend with hills, poised
      like a slipknot

becoming a noose.
   Unlike punji stakes,
      his traps only snag the heart.

Sometimes he turns in a circle
   until a few faces from Dak To
      track him down.

A dress or scarf in the distance
   can nail him to a dogwood.
      Down below, to his left,

from where the smog rises,
   a small voice reaches his ear
      somehow. No, never mind—

he's halfway back, closer to a ravine,
   going deeper into saw vines,
      in behind White Cove,

following his mind like a dark lover,
   away from car horns & backfire
      where only days are stolen.

When Loneliness Is A Man

Yusef Komunyakaa

Laughing, with a TV's blue-static figures
    dancing through the air at 2 A.M.
with eight empty beer bottles lined up
    on the kitchen table, a full moon
gazing through the opened back door,
    his thick fingers drumming the pink
laminex, singing along with a rock video
    of soft porno, recounting dead friends,
with a tally of all his mistakes
    in front of him, after he's punched
the walls & refrigerator with his fist,
    unable to forget childhood's lonely
grass & nameless flowers & insects,
    crying for his black cat
hit by a car, drawing absent faces
    on the air with his right index finger,
rethinking lost years of a broken marriage
    like a wrecked ship inside a green bottle,
puffing a horn-shaped ceramic pipe,
    dragging his feet across the floor
in a dance with the shadow of a tree
    on a yellow wall, going to the wooden fence
to piss under the sky's marsupial stare,
    walking back in to pop the cap
on his last beer, hugging himself awake,
    picking up a dried wishbone
from the table & snapping it, cursing the world,
    softly whispering his daughter's name,
he disturbs the void that is
    heavy as the heart's clumsy logbook.

At 102, Romance Comes Once a Year

(for Joseph Johnson, Seattle)

COLLEEN J. MCELROY

down in Banyantown where young
girls prance swaybacked
for strangers we hear tell
some folks be rememberin' how
old men used to work till
they nothin' more than corn
cobs of brown skin waitin'
for the holiday sun
to warm them red

upriver houses don't need much
care so the old men sit
by the shore where eddies
of water churn the air fresh
and they can munch over
annual events and how too
many young girls go
bad all th' time now

when hours paint houses sunset
orange, old men who be still tryin'
to learn what the word *retire*
means to somebody who ain't never
been laid off try forgettin'
their strokes and force angry
limbs to stiffly water lawns
while their gummy eyes
watch some woman's skirt sway

no matter where I go, Joseph
they all remind me of you

with your shoeshine stand and 100
birthdays but still not looking
a day over 65 by any real
calendar and as pretty black
as any woman be wantin'
noddin' yes when I whisper
magic names of lost cities:
Montego, Toberua, Titicaca, Tiv
Tupelo, Topeka, Tacoma

Father (Part 1)

HARRYETTE MULLEN

My mother told me that after he left us
and we moved back to Texas,
for weeks whenever she'd take me out
I'd run and grab the pantleg
of any man I saw
(no matter if he was black or white)
shouting, "Daddy, Daddy!

She said the white men
backed away redfaced and stiff.
The black men only laughed.

Father's Day

E. ETHELBERT MILLER

My wife asks
"What's wrong with you again?"

Her words cannot subtract the days
Or nights I have spent looking at her back
Or explain how a year's supply of loving
Is suppose to fit inside a Father's Day card

My son looks at me like a pitcher
Shaking off a sign and wanting to throw the
Hard fast one as he refuses to clean his room
Or take the garbage out

My daughter is long gone
Her body chasing some boy's smile around the corner
And I have grown accustomed to long moments of silence
I seldom answer the telephone or read the mail

But today a letter came from a friend in another city
She wrote to tell me about her garden
And how things are going so well this spring
She reminded me to water my heart

To let love grow through the weeds

Epigrams For My Father

(John Henry Redmond, Sr.)

EUGENE B. REDMOND

I

Fatherlore: papa-rites, daddyhood;
     Run & trapsong: Search & dodgesong.
Steelhammeringman.
Gunbouter; whiskeywarrior.
Nightgod!
Moonballer/brawler grown old.
Slaughterhouse/river mackman:
Hightale teller & totempoleman.

II

Wanderer across waters:
Folkbrilliance & Geniusgrit;
Railraging railsplitter:
Railrage! Railrage!
IC & BM & O & MoPac & Midnight Special:
Freight train . . . . . . bring my daddy back!

III

Stone-story. The story of stone, brokenbricks—
Rocks hurled in pleasure & rage,
Pebbles soft & silent:
Home-dome is a blues-hard head.

IV

45-degree hat, Bulldurham butt bailing from lips;
Gabardine shining shining shining
Above white silk socks—
      satin man
      satin man
      silksure & steelstrong

hammerhold on life
hammerhold on life

V

Sun-son. Stonebone. Blackblitz.
Fatherlore. Struggledeep: Afridark, Afrolark,
      daddydepth—
      Riverbottom song.

To the Father of Me

LAMONT B. STEPTOE

All
the places
your hands
never touched
shout now
of your absence
no pay phones
can reach
your distance
not even
lovers can replace
what never was

Amateur Fighter

for my father

NATASHA TRETHEWEY

What's left is the tiny gold glove
hanging from his key chain. But,
before that, he had come to boxing,

as a boy, out of necessity—one more reason
to stay away from home, go late
to that cold house and dinner alone

in the dim kitchen. Perhaps he learned
just to box a stepfather, then turned
that anger into a prize at the Halifax gym.

Later, in New Orleans, there were the books
he couldn't stop reading. A scholar, his eyes
weakening. Fighting, then, a way to live

dangerously. He'd leave his front tooth out
for pictures so that I might understand
living meant suffering, loss. Really living

meant taking risks, so he swallowed
a cockroach in a bar on a dare, dreamt
of being a bullfighter. And at the gym

on Tchoupitoulas Street, he trained
his fists to pound into a bag
the fury contained in his gentle hands.

The red headgear, hiding his face,
could make me think he was someone else,
that my father was somewhere else, not here

holding his body up to pain.

Reflections on Growing Older

QUINCY TROUPE

eye sit here, now, inside my fast thickening breath
the whites of my catfish eyes, muddy with drink
my roped, rasta hair snaking down in twisted salt & pepper
vines braided from the march of years, pen & ink lines etching
my swollen face, the collected weight of years swelling
around my middle, the fear of it all overloading circuits
here & now with the weariness of tears, coming on in storms
the bounce drained out of my once liquid strut
a stork-like gimpiness there now, stiff as death
my legs climbing steep stairs in protest now, the power gone
slack from when eye once heliocoptered through cheers, hung around
    rims
threaded rainbowing jumpshots, that ripped, popped cords & envious
    peers
gone, now the cockiness of that young, firm flesh
perfect as arrogance & the belief that perpetual hard-ons would swell
forever here, smoldering fire in a gristle's desire, drooping limp now
like wet spaghetti, or noodles, the hammer-head that once shot
    straight in
& ramrod hard into the sucking sweet heat of wondrous women
wears a lugubrious melancholy now, like an old frog wears its knobby
    head
croaking like a lonely malcontent through midnight hours
eye sit here, now, inside my own gathering flesh
thickening into an image of humpty-dumpty
at the edge of a fall, the white of my hubris gone
muddy as mississippi river water
eye feel now the assault of shotgunned years
shortening breath, charlie horses throbbing through cold
tired muscles, slack & loose as frayed, old ropes
slipping from round the neck of an executed memory
see, now, these signals of irreversible breakdowns—
the ruination of my once, perfect flesh—as medals earned

fighting through the holy wars of passage, see them as miracles
of the glory of living breath, pulsating music through my poetry—
syncopating metaphors turned here inside out—
see it all now as the paths taken, the choices made
the loves lost & broken, the loves retained
& the poems lost & found in the dark
beating like drumbeats through the heart

Poem For My Father

for Quincy T. Trouppe, Sr.

QUINCY TROUPE

father, it was an honor to be there, in the dugout with you
the glory of great black men swinging their lives as bats
at tiny white balls burning in at unbelievable speeds
riding up & in & out
a curve breaking down wicked, like a ball falling off a high table
moving away, snaking down, screwing its stitched magic
into chitling circuit air, its comma seams spinning
toward breakdown, dipping, like a hipster
bebopping a knee-dip stride in the charlie parker forties
wrist curling, like a swan's neck
behind a slick black back
cupping an invisible ball of dreams
& you there, father, regal as african obeah man
sculpted out of wood, from a sacred tree of no name no place origin
thick roots branching down into cherokee & someplace else lost
way back in africa, the sap running dry crossing
from north carolina into georgia, inside grandmother mary's womb
who was your mother & had you there in the violence of that red soil
ink blotter news gone now into blood & bone graves
of american blues, sponging rococo
truth long gone as dinosaurs
the agent-oranged landscape of former names
absent of african polysyllables, dry husk consonants there now
in their place, names flat as polluted rivers
& that guitar string smile always snaking across
some virulent american redneck's face
scorching, like atomic heat, mushrooming over nagasaki
& hiroshima, the fever-blistered shadows of it all
inked, as body etchings, into sizzled concrete
but you there, father, through it all, a yardbird solo
riffing on bat & ball glory, breaking down all fabricated myths

of white major-league legends, of who was better than who
beating them at their own crap game with killer bats
as bud powell swung his silence into beauty
of a josh gibson home run skittering across piano keys of bleachers
shattering all manufactured legends up there in lights, struck out
white knights on the risky slippery edge of amazement
awe, the miraculous truth slipping through
steeped & disguised in the blues, confluencing
like the point at the cross
when a fastball hides itself up in a shimmying slider
curve breaking down & away in a wicked sly grin
curved & broken-down like the back of an ass-scratching uncle tom
who like old satchel paige delivering his famed hesitation pitch
before coming back with a high hard fast one, rising
is sometimes slicker, slipping & sliding
& quicker than a professional hitman—
the deadliness of it all, the sudden strike
like that of the brown bomber's short crossing right
or the hook of sugar ray robinson's lightning cobra bite

& you there father through it all, catching rhythms of chono
pozo balls, drumming like cuban conga beats into your catcher's mitt
hard & fast as cool papa bell jumping into bed
before the lights went out

of the old negro baseball league, a promise you were
father, a harbinger, of shock waves, soon come

Baby Boy

Afaa Michael Weaver

Baby Boy is a veteran,
his bad leg, his paunch are scars.
He remembers when South Baltimore
was hell and risk for blacks at night;
he has rolled the world to snake eyes
on the black side of Pigtown bars.
Sweat creeps now from fibers of gray hair.
He curls his cigarettes from hidden smiles,
now that the streets are safe to walk
with small twenty-twos and straight razors,
now that black folk are not playthings,
now that curses come from under breath,
as fire snorting from deep down like a snake.
Baby Boy outstrips the youngsters, loading
trucks, soaked in his own water, limping.
Now that we don't have to hold back,
Baby Boy goes through Pigtown in a new car,
his cap turned sideways and down, for business.
Baby Boy is a warrior.

Anatomy

KEVIN YOUNG

1.

deep
in the heart
of the house
the women cook
sweet breads and
simmer

2.

outside
cold dogs are beaten
by my uncles from
the drowsy porch   back
into the arms
of the strong rain
which drove
them there   will
drive them back
again   to the men who claim
this slanted porch
who drink watered wine

3.

the lawn
is covered with cars which
slowly burn   tall grasses rise
smoke from each rusty
engine's fire
my great
grandfather looks out
at barren pecan
trees   he nods
    I call those male
    he coughs
    cause they can't grow
    nothing
    at all

10.

WHOSE CHILDREN ARE THESE?

Whose Children Are These?

GERALD BARRAX

I

Whose children are these?
Who do these children belong to?
With no power to watch over,
He looks at them, sleeping,
Exhaustion overwhelming hunger,
Barely protected with burlap from the cold
Cabin. Fear and rage make him tremble
For them; for himself, shame that he can do no more
Than die for them,
For no certain purpose. He heard about the woman,
Margaret Garner, in spite of the white folks' silence.
How she killed two of hers
To keep them from being taken back;
killed herself after the others were taken back
Anyway. So she saved
Two. He couldn't save his Ellen and Henry.
Who do these belong to?
He doesn't dare kiss them
Now, but stands dreaming,
Willing these five back
To a place or forward to a time
He can't remember or imagine.
All he can do is find the place
He knows about. Leave now

Before dawn sets the white fields raging
And murders the North Star.

II

Grandsire, I kissed, blessed, chewed, and swallowed your rage
when I stood over the five you sent, warm in their beds,
and force-fed my stunned dumb soul to believe someone
owned, someone bought, someone sold at will
our children, Grandsire, I held them, I held them
as you could not, and revered that fierce mother
whose courage and whose solution I could not.
But we have not rescued them altogether;
we moved them through one dimension, from one killing
field to another on history's flat page,
1850s' slavery to 1980s' racism and murder.
Baraka has told us "They have made
this star unsafe, and this age, primitive,"
and it is so. I have stood over each child sleeping
and looked at each child and wanted to know
who decides to break our hearts one by one by one.
The Greeks named it Tyche and made a goddess of chance.
Here they call it this god's mysterious Will.
I have the children, but we have not saved them
from this primitive star, and I am unable to forgive.

the children of the poor (1)

GWENDOLYN BROOKS

People who have no children can be hard:
Attain a mail of ice and insolence:
Need not pause in the fire, and in no sense
Hesitate in the hurricane to guard.
And when wide world is bitten and bewarred
They perish purely, waving their spirits hence
Without a trace of grace or of offense
To laugh or fail, diffident, wonder-starred.
While through a throttling dark we others hear
The little lifting helplessness, the queer
Whimper-whine; whose unridiculous
Lost softness softly makes a trap for us.
And makes a curse. And makes a sugar of
The malocclusions, the inconditions of love.

photograph

*my grandsons
spinning in their joy*

LUCILLE CLIFTON

universe
keep them turning   turning
black blurs against the window
of the world
for they are beautiful
and there is trouble coming
round and round and round

The Furious Boy

TOI DERRICOTTE

In the classroom, the furious boy—a heavy star.
The unhappiness in the room finds his heart,
          enters it;
The sheet of paper flapping in his face.
Who takes something takes it from him.

The rejections look for him
The inflicted pain finds him.
He cannot say no. The hole in his heart deepens,
pain has no way out. A light too heavy
to escape, a presence more concentrated,
warmth is everywhere except where he sits at the center
holding the world in place.
The children touch him gently; the teacher lets him be.
                    Such a weight!
One black child in a perfect town;
there is no reason for sadness.

After Reading *Mickey in the Night Kitchen* for the Third Time Before Bed

I'm in the milk and the milk's in me! . . . I'm Mickey!

RITA DOVE

My daughter spreads her legs
to find her vagina:
hairless, this mistaken
bit of nomenclature
is what a stranger cannot touch
without her yelling. She demands
to see mine and momentarily
we're a lopsided star
among the spilled toys,
my prodigious scallops
exposed to her neat cameo.

And yet the same glazed
tunnel, layered sequences.
She is three; that makes this
innocent. *We're pink!*
she shrieks, and bounds off.

Every month she wants
to know where it hurts
and what the wrinkled string means
between my legs. *This is good blood*
I say, but that's wrong, too.
How to tell her that it's what makes us—
black mother, cream child.
That we're in the pink
and the pink's in us.

Fourteen

JAMES A. EMANUEL

Something is breaking loose,
    leapfrog-straddling kitchen chair,
    slamdown-toss-up at the mouth,
    joke-dropping sloshings
    stepped on, smeared
    with shoelace dragging
    grinning to himself at

Something almost free and hugging;
    unbroken doors agape behind him
    gasp, and bannisters are lurching
    bending up the stairsteps three-in-one
    he skims, punching a grab of cake
    through jacket sleeve and out again
    caught in his snatched-up cap
    and bounding down again, doors
    standing back.

Upstart train of him is loading,
    whistle-steaming,
    squirting clouds,
    taking precious attic rubbish,
    basement-cornered leaning things . . .

You bundle on a stick
    sneakering by,
    unbroken punch of cake,
    where do you think—oh, think—
    you are going?

Nikki-Rosa

Nikki Giovanni

childhood remembrances are always a drag
if you're Black
you always remember things like living in Woodlawn
with no inside toilet
and if you become famous or something
they never talk about how happy you were to have
your mother
all to yourself and
how good the water felt when you got your bath
from one of those
big tubs that folk in chicago barbecue in
and somehow when you talk about home
it never gets across how much you
understood their feelings
as the whole family attended meetings about Hollydale
and even though you remember
your biographers never understand
your father's pain as he sells his stock
and another dream goes
And though you're poor it isn't poverty that
concerns you
and though they fought a lot
it isn't your father's drinking that makes any difference
but only that everybody is together and you
and your sister have happy birthdays and very good
Christmasses
and I really hope no white person ever has cause
to write about me
because they never understand
Black love is Black wealth and they'll
probably talk about my hard childhood
and never understand that
all the while I was quite happy

Black Cryptogram

for Sterling A. Brown

MICHAEL S. HARPER

When God
created
the black child
He was
showing off.

My Children

Lance Jeffers

What children can solve the equation of loveliness
more quickly than these, the abundancies of good?
How like a gifty moon that crosses its legs upon my porch
is the laughter of these children at their father-clown!
How unguent and leafy is their thought!

I will give you whatever blackness you require;
my flesh will be a breakfast for your need,
for you will bring from your loins a race
of saints: dark when they cleave the devil's soul.

Motherhood

GEORGIA DOUGLAS JOHNSON

Don't knock on my door, little child,
I cannot let you in;
You know not what a world this is
Of cruelty and sin.
Wait in the still eternity
Until I come to you.
The world is cruel, cruel, child,
I cannot let you through.

Don't knock at my heart, little one,
I cannot bear the pain
Of turning deaf ears to your call,
Time and time again.
You do not know the monster men
Inhabiting the earth.
Be still, be still, my precious child,
I cannot give you birth.

Circling the Daughter
for Tandi

ETHERIDGE KNIGHT

You came / to be / in the Month of Malcolm,
And the rain fell with a fierce gentleness,
Like a martyr's tears,
On the streets of Manhattan when your light was lit;
And the City sang you Welcome. Now I sit,
Trembling in your presence. Fourteen years
Have brought the moon-blood, the roundness,
The girl-giggles, the grand-leaps.
We are touch-tender in our fears.

You break my eyes with your beauty:
Ooouu-oo-baby-I-love-you.

Do not listen to the lies of old men
Who fear your power,
Who preach that you were "born in sin."
A flower is moral by its own flowering.
Reach always within
For the Music and the Dance and the Circling.

O Tandiwe, by Beloved of this land,
Your spring will come early and
When the earth begins its humming,
Begin your dance with men
With a Grin and a Grace of whirling.
Your place is neither ahead nor behind,
Neither right nor left. The world is round.
Make the sound of your breathing
A silver bell at midnight
And the chilling wet of the morning dew . . .

You break my eyes with your beauty:
Ooouu-oo-baby-I-love-you.

Little Man Around the House

for Ladarius

YUSEF KOMUNYAKAA

Mama Elsie's ninety now.
She calls you whippersnapper.
When you two laugh, her rheumatism
Slips out the window like the burglar
She hears nightly. Three husbands
& an only son dead, she says
I'll always be a daddy's girl.
Sometimes I can't get Papa's face
Outta my head. But this boy, my great-
Great-grandson, he's sugar in my coffee.

You look up from your toy
Telescope, with Satchmo's eyes,
As if I'd put a horn to your lips.
You love maps of buried treasure,
Praying Mantis, & Public Enemy . . .
Blessed. For a moment, I'm jealous.
You sit like the king of trumpet
Between my grandmama & wife,
Youngblood, a Cheshire cat
Hoodooing two birds at once.

Now That I Am Forever with Child

AUDRE LORDE

How the days went
while you were blooming within me
I remember   each upon each
the swelling changed planes of my body

how you first fluttered   then jumped
and I thought it was my heart.

How the days wound down
and the turning of winter
I recall   you
growing heavy against the wind.
I thought   now her hands
are formed   her hair
has started to curl
now her teeth are done
now she sneezes.

Then the seed opened.
I bore you one morning
just before spring
my head rang like a fiery piston
my legs were towers between which
a new world was passing.

Since then
I can only distinguish
one thread within running hours
you   flowing through selves
toward You.

Offspring

NAOMI LONG MADGETT

I tried to tell her:
    This way the twig is bent.
    Born of my trunk and strengthened by my roots,
    You must stretch newgrown branches
    Closer to the sun
    Than I can reach.
I wanted to say:
    Extend my self to that far atmosphere
    Only my dreams allow.

But the twig broke,
And yesterday I saw her
Walking down an unfamiliar street,
    Feet confident,
    Face slanted upward toward a threatening sky,
    And
    She was smiling
    And she was
    Her very free,
    Her very individual,
    Unpliable
    Own.

Accessible Heaven

Thylias Moss

You remember being bathed,
surrendering pink soap
to someone who trusts that your dirt
won't adhere to her own skin.
In a minute a rag is lost to lather.

Terry nubs like taste buds
savor your back and thighs, summoning,
from the six-inch wet depth, your glory.
On the surface of opaque water
is the white conquest of suds
unsullied by what supports their voyage.

You want to watch it forever, risk
pneumonia and croup
just so your hand can be the flotilla's
dark sail. Then her hand
activates the drain, and the holiness
leaves in a vortex.

Not one to spoil you,
she grabs a towel, frisks you,
rubs off everything but the clean
that stays with you
all afternoon.

11.

THEY ARE ALL OF ME

Why Didnt He Tell Me the Whole Truth

AMIRI BARAKA

I'll give you a silver dollar
if you'll learn The Creation.
Why eyes. Big eyes. My mother
had me saying The Gettysburg Address
in a boyscout suit. Why didnt you say
Something else, old man. I never learned
by heart, The Creation, and that is the key
to all life. I strain now through the mists
of other life, to recall that old man's presence.
I know we are linked in destiny and cause.
I know he my guardian and deepest teacher.
I stand on his invisible shoulders.
I look for his enemies to tear their throats.
I wish that he had told me about J. A. Rogers and
Psychopathia Sexualis. I wish he had showed me
his Mason Book.
Perhaps it would have meant another path.
It wda saved some time, some energy, some pain.
But love is the answer we keep saying, only love.
And in my grandfathers pained eyes I remember only
the keen glint of divine magnetism. My grandfather
loved me.

In My Father's House

GEORGE BARLOW

Always first to rise
he usually slipped into daybreak
like a phantom—heading
(in jacket jeans white socks & loafers)
for Alameda
the drowsy traffic
& buzzing electronics of Naval Air
But he plays a horn
& some mornings caught him
aching with jazz—reeling
in its chemistry & might:
Duke Bird Basie
riffs chords changes
softly grunted & mouthed
in his closet
in the hallway in
all the glory of the sunrise

Who knows what spirits
shimmer through the neurons
& acoustics of his sleep
before these mornings:
black Beethoven
shunning his own deafness
for the sake of symphony
a Haitian drummer—
eyes shut in the moonlight—
mounted by divine horsemen
who flash through his hands
pretty Billie
eating gardenias with a needle
singing the blues away

Maybe urges older than oceans
startle him in the shower
or in the livingroom
on his way out the door
compel him to swipe moments
from time he doesn't have
to inch notes across
pitiless lined sheets
that have waited on the piano all night
for beat & harmony to marry

On these mornings
he met the man with ease
didn't carry no heavy load
Car horns were trumpets
fog horns bassoons
train whistles blushing saxophones
On these mornings
he jammed with angels
popped his fingers
to music in his head
filled his great lungs
with cool air

Kitchenette Building

Gwendolyn Brooks

We are things of dry hours and the involuntary plan,
Grayed in, and gray. "Dream" makes a giddy sound, not strong
Like "rent," "feeding a wife," "satisfying a man."

But could a dream send up through onion fumes
Its white and violet, fight with fried potatoes
And yesterday's garbage ripening in the hall,
Flutter, or sing an aria down these rooms

Even if we were willing to let it in,
Had time to warm it, keep it very clean,
Anticipate a message, let it begin?

We wonder. But not well! not for a minute!
Since Number Five is out of the bathroom now,
We think of lukewarm water, hope to get in it.

Cousin Mary

Wanda Coleman

goes way back to the days / my father a young man

central avenue his pride that tore down cobalt blue
plymouth struggle buggy and mom slave
to the sewing machine

pops used to babysit me / take me for rides everywhere
beside him staring out the window at all the black faces
making tracks
that was where the cotton club used to be
and the bucket of blood. do you remember when
nat king cole played on the avenue and
the dunbar hotel where all the high steppers
went
saturday night like after the joe louis fight or on leave
from washing down the latrines of world war two
at the chicken shack greasin' down
with the black stars

that was before "we" had tv and pops was hot stuff
selling insurance. used to take me everywhere
i was *his* little girl (till baby brother got big enough)

we used to climb stairs / big stairs at golden state insurance
and my dad important, suit and tie—would prop me
up on his desk and the office people would
come around and say how pretty i was
all done up in pale pink organdy with taffeta ribbons to match
pink thin cotton socks and white patent leather shoes

she goes way back / those days / wide-eyed impressions

pops would take me to visit
her dancing with the gis / boogie-woogie'n to

some dap daddy ticklin' ivories on the spin of a 78
playing cards and talking that talk

me a little bundle of grins
looking up at all those adults/trying to swallow it all
with my eyes. she was so fine
a warm friendly smile making her home mine

years later done in—arthritis and bad men
doing for those who can't help themselves and barely able
to help herself. selfless. a beauty so deep
gift of inexpensive ash trays to be remembered by/gold

her song to me across years

Family Secrets

Toi Derricotte

They told my cousin Rowena not to marry
Calvin—she was too young, just eighteen,
& he was too dark, too too dark, as if he
had been washed in what we wanted
to wipe off our hands. Besides, he didn't come
from a good family. He said he was going
to be a lawyer, but we didn't quite believe.
The night they eloped to the Gotham Hotel,
the whole house whispered—as if we were ashamed
to tell it to ourselves. My aunt and uncle
rushed down to the Gotham to plead—
we couldn't imagine his hands on her!
Families are conceived in many ways.
The night my cousin Calvin lay
down on her, that idol with its gold skin
broke, & many of the gods we loved
in secret were freed.

Touching/Not Touching: My Mother

TOI DERRICOTTE

i

That first night in the hotel bedroom,
when the lights go out,
she is already sleeping (that woman who has always
claimed sleeplessness), inside her quiet breathing
like a long red gown. How can she
sleep? My heart beats as if I am alone,
for the first time, with a lover or a beast.
Will I hate her drooping mouth,
her old woman rattle? Once I nearly
suffocated on her breast. Now I can almost
touch the other side of my life.

ii

Undressing
in the dark,
looking,
not looking,
we parade before each other,
old proud peacocks, in our stretch marks
with hanging butts. We are equals. No
more do I need to wear her high heels to step
inside the body of a woman.
Her beauty and strangeness no longer seduce
me out of myself. I show my good side, my
long back, strong mean legs, my thinness that
came from learning to hold back
from taking what's not mine. No more
a thief for love. She takes off her
bra, facing me, and I see those gorgeous
globes, soft, creamy,
high; my mouth waters.
how will I resist
crawling in beside her, putting
my hand for warmth under
her thin night dress?

Taking in Wash

RITA DOVE

Papa called her Pearl when he came home
drunk, swaying as if the wind touched
only him. Towards winter his skin paled,
buckeye to ginger root, cold drawing
the yellow out. The Cherokee in him,
Mama said. Mama never changed:
when the dog crawled under the stove
and the back gate slammed, Mama hid
the laundry. Sheba barked as she barked
in snow or clover, a spoiled and ornery bitch.

She was Papa's girl,
black though she was. Once,
in winter, she walked through a dream
all the way down the stairs
to stop at the mirror, a beast
with stricken eyes
who screamed the house awake. Tonight

every light hums, the kitchen arctic
with sheets. Papa is making the hankies
sail. Her foot upon a silk
stitched rose, she waits
until he turns, his smile sliding all over.
Mama a tight dark fist.
Touch that child

and I'll cut you down
just like the cedar of Lebanon.

Abraham Got All the Stars n the Sand

RUTH FORMAN

Daddy 43 but look 40
35 when he laugh
ma family big n pretty

Bo
look like smooth onyx stone
Randy look like
Florida sand
Winnie
the breath of honeysuckle
Leesha
a redwood tree
Peaches
look like plums
n Momma
sweet coconut meat
next to Daddy color of baking chocolate

n Jojo
she buckwheat honey
in the mornin
when Daddy grease n part her hair
for the ready red ribbons
glow so next to her skin

he
put twists in Leesha's
n Peaches get three thick braids
We always sing
different songs at the table

n Gramma let us do it
as she pour her coffee
watch them lil teeth shinin
thinkin
Abraham got all the stars n the sand
but she got all the rainbow.

Mothers

Nikki Giovanni

the last time i was home
to see my mother we kissed
exchanged pleasantries
and unpleasantries pulled a warm
comforting silence around
us and read separate books

i remember the first time
i consciously saw her
we were living in a three room
apartment on burns avenue

mommy always sat in the dark
i don't know how i knew that but she did

that night i stumbled into the kitchen
maybe because i've always been
a night person or perhaps because i had wet
the bed
she was sitting on a chair
the room was bathed in moonlight diffused through tiny window
        panes
she may have been smoking but maybe not
her hair was three-quarters her height
which made me a strong believer in the samson myth
and very black

i'm sure i just hung there by the door
i remember thinking: what a beautiful lady
she was very deliberately waiting
perhaps for my father to come home
from his night job or maybe for a dream
that had promised to come by

"come here" she said "i'll teach you
a poem: *i see the moon*
      the moon sees me
      god bless the moon
      and good bless me"
i taught that to my son
who recited it for her
just to say we must learn
to bear the pleasures
as we have borne the pains

Knoxville, Tennessee

Nikki Giovanni

I always like summer
best
you can eat fresh corn
from daddy's garden
and okra
and greens
and cabbage
and lots of
barbecue
and buttermilk
and homemade ice cream
at the church picnic
and listen to
gospel music
outside
at the church
homecoming
and go to the mountains with
your grandmother
and go barefooted
and be warm
all the time
not only when you go to bed
and sleep

Camp Story

MICHAEL S. HARPER

I look over the old photos
for the US Hotel fire,
1900 Saratoga Springs,
where your grandfather
was chef on loan
from Catskill
where you were born.

The grapes from his arbor
sing in my mouth:
the smoke from the trestle
of his backyard,
the engine so close
to the bedroom
I can almost touch it,
make bricks from the yards
of perfection,
the clear puddles from the Hudson River,
where you would make change
at the dayline,
keep the change from the five
Jackleg Diamonds would leave
on the counter top or the stool.

Where is the CCC camp
you labored in
to send the money home to the family,
giving up your scholarship
so you could save the family
homestead from the banks of the river.

All across America the refugees
find homes in these camps

and are made to eat
at a table of liberty
you could have had
if you could not spell
or count, or keep time.

I see you, silent, wordfully
talking to my brother, Jonathan,
as he labors on the chromatic
respirator; you kiss his brown
temple where his helmet left
a slight depression
near a neat line of stitches
at the back of his skull.

As he twitches to chemicals
the Asian nurses catheter
into the cavities and caves
of his throat and lungs:
the doctor repeats the story
of his chances.

Kin 2

—one more time—(unblue version)
for Shirl

MICHAEL S. HARPER

When news came that your mother'd
smashed her hip, both feet caught
in rungs of the banquet table,
our wedding rebroken on the memory
of the long lake of silence
when the stones of her body
broke as an Irish fence of stones,
I see your wet dugs drag
with the weight of our daughter
in the quick of her sleep
to another feeding.

I pick you up from the floor
of your ringing fears, the floor
where the photographs you have worked
cool into the sky of the gray you love,
and you are back at the compost pile
where the vegetables burn,
or swim in the storm of your childhood,
when your father egged you on with his
open machinery, the exhaust choking your sisters,
and your sisters choked still.

Now the years pile up on themselves,
and his voice stops you in accusation,
in the eggs of your stretched sons,
one born on his birthday, both dead.
I pull you off into the sanctuary
of conciliation, of quiet tactics,
the uttered question, the referral,
which will quiet the condition you have seen
in your mother's shadow, the crutches
inching in the uncut grass,
and the worn body you will carry
as your own birthmark of his scream.

Those Winter Sundays

Robert Hayden

Sundays too my father got up early
and put his clothes on in the blueblack cold,
then with cracked hands that ached
from labor in the weekday weather made
banked fires blaze. No one ever thanked him.

I'd wake and hear the cold splintering, breaking.
When the rooms were warm, he'd call,
and slowly I would rise and dress,
fearing the chronic angers of that house,

Speaking indifferently to him,
who had driven out the cold
and polished my good shoes as well.
What did I know, what did I know
of love's austere and lonely offices?

Big Zeb Johnson

Everett Hoagland

Mother's father:
red brown, raw-boned, Virginia born,
Indian Blood, from whom I get my six/four size,
died of diabetes during the White Depression,
leaving three high-strung, violin colored
daughters and Brotherly Love's widow,
Aunt Tootsie, who I, later, as first born,
manchild, grandchild, named Mama Wawa,
who, also sick with "sugar," wound up
worn out, from taking in the world's wash,
waiting for ". . . that Great Gettin' Up Morning . . ."
with one leg, sweetly mad, in an old
World War One wicker wheelchair and died
of diabetes.

I am because you
unemployed and blue
sugar-blooded, through those old T.B. and pneumonia
times never let the three, not one of their six
small feet, get wet or cold
when the chilling, killing, colorless
flakes fell one, or two, or three feet deep.

You took your knife-edged, steel coal shovel, a pace
ahead of their in-a-row, gosling gait,
and awed eyes gawked, window shades
went up, curtains parted, in witness to such love:
Philly folk watching you dig down to the slate and brick
sidewalks, metal-on-stone sparks and phosphorescent snow,
sun powder, glinting over and around

the fire aura crowning
the big, bent over, upright, steam exhaling, drive-shaft-fast, locomotive
    of a man,
". . . going like sixty . . ."
leaning into the labor, fathering,
fathering, the whole long, cold mile to school:
"Diabetes be damned!"

Your neighbors came to count on this
courtly care, their kids following yours,
all in a row, those retold winter mornings, so many miles
and years ago. Today, the you in me,
through genes and oral history, speaks
of the gray haired rigors of the long haul,
going on sixty, as I deal
with my own three, worrisome, brown sugar, teenaged
daughters—and live
with diabetes.

The Idea of Ancestry

ETHERIDGE KNIGHT

I

Taped to the wall of my cell are 47 pictures: 47 black
faces: my father, mother, grandmothers (1 dead), grand
fathers (both dead), brothers, sisters, uncles, aunts,
cousins (1st & 2nd), nieces, and nephews. They stare
across the space at me sprawling on my bunk. I know
their dark eyes, they know mine. I know their style,
they know mine. I am all of them, they are all of me;
they are farmers, I am a thief, I am me, they are thee.

I have at one time or another been in love with my mother,
1 grandmother, 2 sisters, 2 aunts (1 went to the asylum),
and 5 cousins. I am now in love with a 7 yr old niece
(she sends me letters written in large block print, and
her picture is the only one that smiles at me).

I have the same name as 1 grandfather, 3 cousins, 3 nephews,
and 1 uncle. The uncle disappeared when he was 15, just took
off and caught a freight (they say). He's discussed each year
when the family has a reunion, he causes uneasiness in
the clan, he is an empty space. My father's mother, who is 93
and who keeps the Family Bible with everybody's birth dates
(and death dates) in it, always mentions him. There is no
place in her Bible for "whereabouts unknown."

II

Each Fall the graves of my grandfathers call me, the brown
hills and red gullies of mississippi send out their electric
messages, galvanizing my genes. Last yr/like a salmon quitting
the cold ocean—leaping and bucking up his birthstream /I
hitchhiked my way from L.A. with 16 caps in my pocket and a
monkey on my back, and I almost kicked it with the kinfolks.
I walked barefooted in my grandmother's backyard /I smelled the

old land and the woods/I sipped cornwhiskey from fruit jars with the
    men /
I flirted with the women/I had a ball till the caps ran out
and my habit came down. That night I looked at my grandmother
and split/my guts were screaming for junk /but I was almost
contented/I had almost caught up with me.
    The next day in Memphis I cracked a croaker's crib for a fix.

This yr there is a gray stone wall damming my stream, and when
the falling leaves stir my genes, I pace my cell or flop on my bunk
and stare at 47 black faces across the space. I am all of them,
they are all of me, I am me, they are thee, and I have no sons
to float in the space between.

My Father's Loveletters

Yusef Komunyakaa

On Fridays he'd open a can of Jax
After coming home from the mill,
& ask me to write a letter to my mother
Who sent postcards of desert flowers
Taller than men. He would beg,
Promising to never beat her
Again. Somehow I was happy
She had gone, & sometimes wanted
To slip in a reminder, how Mary Lou
Williams's "Polka Dots & Moonbeams"
Never made the swelling go down.
His carpenter's apron always bulged
With old nails, a claw hammer
Looped at his side & extension cords
Coiled around his feet.
Words rolled from under the pressure
Of my ballpoint: Love,
Baby, Honey, Please.

We sat in the quiet brutality
Of voltage meters & pipe threaders,
Lost between sentences . . .
The gleam of a five-pound wedge
On the concrete floor
Pulled a sunset
Through the doorway of his toolshed.
I wondered if she laughed
& held them over a gas burner.
My father could only sign
His name, but he'd look at blueprints
& say how many bricks
Formed each wall. This man,
Who stole roses & hyacinth
For his yard, would stand there
With eyes closed & fists balled,
Laboring over a simple word, almost
Redeemed by what he tried to say.

Black Mother Woman

AUDRE LORDE

I cannot recall you gentle
yet through your heavy love
I have become
an image of your once-delicate flesh
split with deceitful longings.

When strangers come and compliment me
your aged spirit takes a bow
jingling with pride
but once you hid that secret
in the center of your fury
hanging me
with deep breasts and wiry hair
your own split flesh
and long-suffering eyes
buried in myths of little worth.

But I have peeled away your anger
down to its core of love
and look mother
I am   a dark temple
where your true spirit rises
beautiful   tough as chestnut
stanchion against nightmares of weakness
and if my eyes conceal
a squadron of conflicting rebellions
I learned from you
to define myself
through your denials.

Under the Oak Table

COLLEEN J. McELROY

I sit crotch high
   Scenting the heavy fat
   Of my ancestry,
Hearing stories of the Lord
   And ditch niggers
Both coming in from the South.

The heavy oak of table legs
   Doubled in pairs
   By oak legs of Mama's sisters,
As I hide in a private jungle
   Viewing the underside
Of table and kin.

Subjects of sin are whispered,
   But my ears are large
   Under the shroud of legs.
Brother, never mentioned without
   His hooked nose,
Refuses an invitation to tea.

This time I'll count wooden legs,
   And try not to sneeze away
   Five reasons Uncle Roman's son died.
A spider chooses the wrong leg,
   And I prepare him for burial
As Brother's wife is inspected—blood will tell.

A dozen times in one afternoon
   They relive the deaths
   Of favorite sisters, Fannie and Jessie.
Fannie looked like Mama.

Soda pop and peckerwoods
Come in all flavors, some too sweet.

Kidney stew and dumplings mingle
With the smell of musk and oak.
While Claudia, head hauncho,
Takes her seat. Don't ask her twice;
The biggest sister of them all,
And Mama leads the yes chorus.

Ruth

*And Ruth said . . . Intreat me not to leave thee, or to return
from following after thee; for whither thou goest, I will go . . .*
—Ruth 1:16

COLLEEN J. MCELROY

it took 27 years to write this poem
27 years mama and still I see you falling
like a lump of coal down a chute
arms hands and feathered thighs churning
inside a tumbling hulk of helpless flesh
falling away from me
your dress flying open
until you were finally free form
and without face

since then I have counted those stairs
I would like to say there were 27
but significance lies not in exactness
but in the panic of not knowing
which step would claim you
I have saved that morning
the blood-sucking thud of body
against wood   the back staircase
of that red brick duplex
where you clawed air

we had fought   I remember that
about what   nothing
grandpa's untimely death
my 16-year-old womanish ways
how someday I too would flail
at my own daughter
so many fights   so many stairs
and you tumbling as my terror

claimed me like Venus
without arms or legs to stop you

one moment you were larger than life
your black arms spread like the wings
of some great vulture   the next a step
missed and you fragile   distorted   plunging
in wingless flight toward some evil nucleus
waiting in the space below the steps
but we cannot go back
I cannot correct that split second
when I failed to lean forward
bodies will not reverse and tumble
upward   unwinding into familiar forms
limbs intact   I have hesitated too long
and the landing is too crowded

what dusty things we would find there now
how you quoted Shakespeare for every event
from slamming doors to Sunday walks and bigotry
a broken lamp   your jealousy and mine
too many unspoken holidays
for your one daughter too many
or too many husbands for one daughter
how your senseless plunge into a void
showed me more than all your ominous warnings
how the cycle of blood and pain
has brought us both to this childless time

I have finally faced myself in you
for years I have written poems nonstop
but yours were always more difficult
I have even tried dream language
but your image slips into some zone
of blackness even deeper in color
than your skin when I angered you
how often has the venom from your blueberry
lips stunted the growth of a poem
how often has your voice been with me
wherever I go   you have gone

and sometimes gladly my need to reach out
has pulled you to me
mama for years I have hidden
hundreds of unfinished verses
in the corners of dark closets
read this
and count them

Jasmine

E. ETHELBERT MILLER

on my desk is a small bottle
which once held perfume
inside is the cord that joined
my wife and daughter

it is strange that i keep it

my mother kept my brother's
sixth finger in a jar stuffed
with cotton

one night i found it
while secretly searching
for cookies hidden in a drawer
filled with underwear
why do we keep things that are not ours?

in another land
an old woman would take this cord
and place it in the earth

tomorrow when my daughter becomes a woman
i will give her this small bottle
filled with the beginnings of herself

on that day she will hold love
in her hands

One for All Newborns

Thylias Moss

They kick and flail like crabs on their backs.
Parents outside the nursery window do not believe
they might raise assassins or thieves, at the very worst
a poet or obscure jazz musician whose politics
spill loudly from his horn.
Everything about it was wonderful, the method
of conception, the gestation, the womb opening
in perfect analogy to the mind's expansion.
Then the dark succession of constricting years,
mother competing with daughter for beauty and losing,
varicose veins and hot-water bottles, joy boiled away,
the arrival of knowledge that eyes are birds with clipped wings,
the sun at a 30° angle and unable to go higher, parents
who cannot push anymore, who stay by the window
looking for signs of spring
and the less familiar gait of grown progeny.
I am now at the age where I must begin to pay
for the way I treated my mother. My daughter is just like me.
The long trip home is further delayed, my presence
keeps the plane on the ground. If I get off, it will fly.
The propeller is a cross spinning like a buzz saw
about to cut through me. I am haunted and my mother is not dead.
The miracle was not birth but that I lived despite my crimes.
I treated God badly also; he is another parent
watching his kids through a window, eager to be proud
of his creation, looking for signs of spring.

Saturday Afternoon, When Chores Are Done

Harryette Mullen

I've cleaned house
and the kitchen smells like pine.
I can hear the kids yelling
through the back screen door.
While they play tug-of-war
with an old jumprope
and while these blackeyed peas
boil on the stove,
I'm gonna sit here at the table
and plait my hair.

I oil my hair and brush it soft.
Then, with the brush in my lap,
I gather the hair in my hands,
pull the strands smooth and tight,
and weave three sections into a fat shiny braid
that hangs straight down my back.

I remember mama teaching me to plait my hair
one Saturday afternoon when chores were done.
My fingers were stubby and short.
I could barely hold three strands at once,
and my braids would fray apart
no sooner than I'd finished them.
Mama said, "Just takes practice, is all."
Now my hands work swiftly, doing easily
what was once so hard to do.

Between time on the job,
keeping house, and raising two girls by myself,
there's never much time like this,
for thinking and being alone.
Time to gather life together

before it unravels like an old jump rope
and comes apart at the ends.

Suddenly I notice the silence.
The noisy tug-of-war has stopped.
I get up to check out back,
see what my girls are up to now.
I look out over the kitchen sink,
where the sweet potato plant
spreads green in the window.
They sit quietly on the back porch steps,
   Melinda plaiting Carla's hair
into a crooked braid.

Older daughter,
you are learning what I am learning:
to gather the strands together
with strong fingers,
to keep what we do
from coming apart at the ends.

a poem for my father

SONIA SANCHEZ

how sad it must be
to love so many women
to need so many black
perfumed bodies weeping
underneath you.
                   when i remember all those nights
i filled my mind with
long wars between short
sighted trojans & greeks
while you slapped some
wide hips about in
your pvt dungeon,
when i remember your
deformity   i want to
do something about your
makeshift manhood.
i guess
        that is why
on meeting your sixth
wife, i cross myself
with her confessionals.

Little Girl Talk

Delores S. Williams

my grampaw was a smooth black, way back then
before black discovered beautiful he was pretty.
he had pearlywhite teeth and a big mustache
he useta skinny-out to the edge with a black-wax stick.
on sunday he would pindown in his darkblue suit, wideblue
tie. white-stiff shirt, and hip-on down to the presbyterian church
where he argued over how to spend
white folk's mission money.

on weekdays: overalls. he worked in a factory.
until some white boss talked down to him. then he'd quit.
to another factory. talk union talk to negroes. get
laid off. on the way home buy me a big box of kran
kause i kalled iron 'i-roan'.

my grampaw was all the kings i wanted to know. when
i was six. my grampaw was smart. didn't
go to college. said white folks wouldn't let'im.
but he worked algebra and trig and read gladstone's law
and science books. he used to tell us kids
there wasn't no heaven.

my grampaw said i was the sugar in his coffee. yes indeed,
i remember my grampaw,

the day the siren screamed into our street ballgame
and stopped at our house, we kids, eight of us, scattered
into an uneven line across the street. we watched two
big, redneck, white men in white uniforms stuff my
pretty grampaw into something called a straitjacket,
crowd him into the back of their looneywagon, jump
into the front themselves and shriek-off into the distance.
my grammaw stood perfectly still. her proud eyes

looked deep and sore and hollow. my mother, unmoving, cried softly.
i, girl-boy-tom-tree-climber of 10, tried
not to feel anything. the tears that didn't come swelled
to a tight fist in my chest

big, brave, girlboy me
shoved the weight of my ten years
onto two flat feet,
strolled to the middle of the street
and yelled as loud as i could,
"throw the ball, shity!"
    The game was on.

If he let us go now

SHERLEY ANNE WILLIAMS

        let me strap
the baby in the seat, just don't say
nothin all that while . . .
                 I move round to
the driver side of the car. The air
warm and dry here. Lawd know what it be
in L.A. He open the door for me
and I slide behind the wheel. Baby
facin me lookin without even
blinkin his eye. I wonder if he
know I'm his mamma that I love him
that that his daddy by the door (and
he won't let us go; he still got time
to say wait. Baby blink once but
he only five week old and whatever
he know don't show.
            His daddy call
my name and I turn to him and wait.
It be cold in the Grapevine at night
this time of year. Wind come whistlin down
through them mountains almost blow this old
VW off the road. I'll be in
touch he say. Say, take care; say, write if
you need somethin.
              I *will* him to touch
us now, to take care us, to know what
we need is him and his name. He slap
the car door, say, drive careful and turn
to go. If he let us go now . . . how
we gon ever take him back? I ease
out on the clutch, mash in on the gas.
The only answer I get is his back.

The Boiling

KEVIN YOUNG

My grandfather wore white
suits, would hitch up his favorite
white pony & head to town,
waving his hat like ivory dice,
a small fortune. Even
white folks called him
Mister. Mama had his dark

knuckles, passed down
from Great Mother's set
of black children—with them
she carried seasons & filled
stomachs, lowering that big black
pot perched high on the shelf:

come autumn she boiled
an army's worth of gumbo,
more bone than chicken
lilting up from the mud-
colored broth; summers
that pot fixed all
the crawdads we caught

along the road's shoulder, claws sunk
into leftovers, into meat cubes
strung to sticks. Once a year
maybe turtle soup. After the holiday
hog went, you had two choices
& that one pot: leave the fat
on the skin to skillet up squat

hourglasses of sweet cracklin,
downing it with ginger sauce;

or slice the fat off & stir
& stir till it passed for soap.
No one ever bathed with that,
mind you, our backsides saw
Lifebuoy like anybody else's.

Hogsoap got saved for washday,
each week the dark pot descending
like some Jesus to the stove, filling up
with lye as we cleaned our Sunday
best, clothes simmering, churned
then beaten good & white.

12

Oh, singing tree!

Ma Rainey

Sterling A. Brown

I

When Ma Rainey
Comes to town,
Folks from anyplace
Miles aroun',
From Cape Girardeau,
Poplar Bluff,
Flocks in to hear
Ma do her stuff;
Comes flivverin' in,
Or ridin' mules,
Or packed in trains,
Picknickin' fools. . . .
That's what it's like,
Fo' miles on down,
To New Orleans delta
An' Mobile town,
When Ma hits
Anywheres aroun'.

II

Dey comes to hear Ma Rainey from de little river settlements,
From blackbottom cornrows and from lumber camps;
Dey stumble in de hall, jes a-laughin' an' a-cacklin',
Cheerin' lak roarin' water, lak wind in river swamps.

An' some jokers keeps deir laughs a-goin' in de crowded aisles,
An' some folks sits dere waitin' wid deir aches an' miseries,
Till Ma comes out before dem, a-smilin' gold-toofed smiles
An' Long Boy ripples minors on de black an' yellow keys.

III

O Ma Rainey,
Sing yo' song;
Now you's back
Whah you belong,
Git way inside us,
Keep us strong. . . .
O Ma Rainey,
Li'l an' low;
Sing us 'bout de hard luck
Roun' our do';
Sing us 'bout de lonesome road
We mus' go. . . .

IV

I talked to a fellow, an' the fellow say,
"She jes' catch hold of us, somekindaway.
She sang Backwater Blues one day:
    'It rained fo' days an' de skies was dark as night,
    Trouble taken place in de lowlands at night.

    'Thundered an' lightened an' the storm begin to roll
    Thousan's of people ain't got no place to go.

    'Den I went an' stood upon some high ol' lonesome hill,
    An' looked down on the place where I used to live.'

An' den de folks, dey natchally bowed dey heads an' cried,
Bowed dey heavy heads, shet dey moufs up tight an' cried,
An' Ma lef' de stage, an' followed some de folks outside."

Dere wasn't much more de fellow say:
She jes' gits hold of us dataway.

Hell Hound Blues

Got to keep movin'
Got to keep movin'
Hell hound on my trail.

D. L. CROCKETT-SMITH

In Robert Johnson's blue song
foreboding follows implacably,
hidden in every shadow, every wind,
palpable as breath, yet unnameable
except as metaphor. Palpable
as a guitar chord or a switchblade
in the heart. Real as a man's moan.
Unnameable as the woman Johnson
loved—the one who fed him poison.

Brother John

for John O. Stewart

MICHAEL S. HARPER

Black man:
I'm a black man;
I'm black; I am—
A black man; black—
I'm a black man;
I'm a black man;
I'm a man; black—
I am—

Bird, buttermilk bird—
smack, booze and bitches
I am Bird
baddest nightdreamer
on sax in the ornithology-world
I can fly—higher, high, higher—
I'm a black man;
I am; I'm a black man—

Miles, blue haze,
Miles high, another bird,
more Miles, mute,
Mute Miles, clean,
bug-eyed, unspeakable,
Miles, sweet Mute,
sweat Miles, black Miles;
I'm a black man;
I'm black; I am;
I'm a black man—

Trane, Coltrane; John Coltrane;
it's tranetime; chase the Trane;

it's a slow dance;
it's the Trane
in Alabama; acknowledgement,
a love supreme,
it's black Trane; black;
I'm a black man; I'm black;
I am; I'm a black man—

Brother John, Brother John
plays no instrument;
he's a black man; black;
he's a black man; he is
Brother John; Brother John—

I'm a black man; I am;
black; I am; I'm a black
man; I am; I am;
I'm a black man;
I'm a black man;
I am; I'm a black man;
I am:

Homage to the Empress of the Blues

ROBERT HAYDEN

Because there was a man somewhere in a candystripe silk shirt,
gracile and dangerous as a jaguar and because a woman moaned
for him in sixty-watt gloom and mourned him Faithless Love
Twotiming Love Oh Love Oh Careless Aggravating Love,

    She came out on the stage in yards of pearls, emerging like
    a favorite scenic view, flashed her golden smile and sang.

Because grey laths began somewhere to show from underneath
torn hurdygurdy lithographs of dollfaced heaven;
and because there were those who feared alarming fists of snow
on the door and those who feared the riot-squad of statistics,

    She came out on the stage in ostrich feathers, beaded satin,
    and shone that smile on us and sang.

Jazzonia

Langston Hughes

O, silver tree!
Oh, shining rivers of the soul!

In a Harlem cabaret
Six long-headed jazzers play.
A dancing girl whose eyes are bold
Lifts high a dress of silken gold.

Oh, singing tree!
Oh, shining rivers of the soul!

Were Eve's eyes
In the first garden
Just a bit too bold?
Was Cleopatra gorgeous
In a gown of gold?

Oh, shining tree!
Oh, silver rivers of the soul!

In a whirling cabaret
Six long-headed jazzers play.

Walking Parker Home

BOB KAUFMAN

Sweet beats of jazz impaled on slivers of wind
Kansas Black Morning/ First Horn Eyes/
Historical sound pictures on New Bird wings
People shouts/boy alto dreams/ Tomorrow's
Gold belled pipe of stops and future Blues Times
Lurking Hawkins/shadows of Lester/ realization
Bronze fingers—brain extensions seeking trapped sounds
Ghetto thoughts/bandstand courage/ solo flight
Nerve-wracked suspicions of newer songs and doubts
New York altar city/black tears/ secret disciples
Hammer horn pounding soul marks on unswinging gates
Culture gods/mob sounds/visions of spikes
Panic excursions to tribal Jazz wombs and transfusions
Heroin nights of birth/and soaring/over boppy new ground.
Smothered rage covering pyramids of notes spontaneously exploding
Cool revelations/shrill hopes/beauty speared into greedy ears
Birdland   nights on bop mountains, windy saxophone revolutions
Dayrooms of junk/and melting walls and circling vultures/
Money cancer/remembered pain/terror flights/
Death and indestructible existence

In that Jazz corner of life
Wrapped in a mist of sound
His legacy, our Jazz-tinted dawn
Wailing his triumphs of oddly begotten dreams
Inviting the nerveless to feel once more
That fierce dying of humans consumed
In raging fires of Love.

Copacetic Mingus

" 'Mingus One, Two and Three.
Which is the image you want the world to see?' "
—Charles Mingus, *Beneath the Underdog*

YUSEF KOMUNYAKAA

Heartstring. Blessed wood
& every moment the thing's made of:
ball of fatback
licked by fingers of fire.
Hard love, it's hard love.
Running big hands down
the upright's wide hips,
rocking his moon-eyed mistress
with gold in her teeth.
Art & life bleed
into each other
as he works the bow.
But tonight we're both a long ways
from the Mile High City,
1973. Here in New Orleans
years below sea level,
I listen to *Pithecanthropus*
Erectus: Up & down, under
& over, every which way—
thump, thump, dada—ah, yes.
Wood heavy with tenderness,
Mingus fingers the loom
gone on Segovia,
dogging the raw strings
unwaxed with rosin.
Hyperbolic bass line. Oh, no!
Hard love, it's hard love.

Glenn on Monk's Mountain

—"mu" twenty-fourth part—

NATHANIEL MACKEY

Next it was Austria we
were in. Unexpected rain
  soaked our shoes,
unexpected snow froze
                  our
   feet. A bitter book
  took us there . . .
               A bitter
book in our stomachs,
   an aftertaste on
  our tongues, a book
             based
  on another Glenn,
           Monk's
Mountain not the Monk's we
  took it for. A book of overlay,
a book about death at fifty-one,
               a book
we lay awake at night reading,
  a book we read wanting
  to wake up from . . .
            So it
  was another Monk's
Mountain we haunted. Sat
             upside
it crosslegged, lotusheaded,
             humphed,
  heads encased in crystal it
 seemed . . . Bits of straw like
  unexpected snow filled the
               sky.
Stars were bits of straw blown

about in the crystal we were
    in, the rags on our backs a bolt
    of black, star-studded
                                cloth,
    the jukebox dressed us in
gabardine, burlap, scratched
    our skin with raw silk . . .

A bit of straw caught in my eye
    made it water,   water
                                filled my
    head with salt . . . Straw, ridden
by water, filled my head, my
throat, my chest,   salt filled
    my head with sound. A sound of
                                bells

    not of bells but of pounded
iron, the Falasha spoken to
    by Ogun . . . I played "Asaph,"
the horn's bell a swung censer,
                                wafted
    scent the furtive sound I sought . . .
Liturgical ambush . . . Fugitive straw . . .
Limbic ambush . . . Nastic address . . .
    Pads and keys cried out for
        climb, clamor, something yet
                                to arrive
we called rung. Rickety wood, split
    reed, sprung ladder. More splinters
the more steps we took . . . Rung
    was a bough made of air, an
unlikely plank suddenly under our
                                feet we
floated up from,   rung was a loquat
    limb, runaway ladder, bent miraculous
branch, thetic step . . . Flesh beginning
    to go like wax, we sat like Buddha,
                                breath
    an abiding chime, chimeless,
                                bells

    had we been
rung

Lamda

Melvin B. Tolson

From the mouth of the Harlem Gallery
    came a voice like a
      ferry horn in a river of fog:

King Oliver of New Orleans
has kicked the bucket, but he left behind
    old Satchmo with his red-hot horn
    to syncopate the heart and mind.
    The honky-tonks in Storyville
have turned to ashes, have turned to dust,
    but old Satchmo is still around
like Uncle Sam's IN GOD WE TRUST.

    Where, oh, where is Bessie Smith
with her heart as big as the blues of truth?
    Where, oh, where is Mister Jelly Roll
    with his Cadillac and diamond tooth?
    Where oh, where is Papa Handy
with his blue notes a-dragging from bar to bar?
    Where, oh, where is bulletproof Leadbelly
    with his tall tales and 12-string guitar?

Dancers

Afaa Michael Weaver

Chick Webb and Billy Strayhorn
moved inside our heads with sound.
They danced with shoes that hit around
invisible points where rhythm is born.

Or they moved like rotund ladies.
A delayed bounce, swish, and sway
rocked you into a melody the way
grand movement entices, empties.

Inside their world of pitch and tone,
Of vibrato and rhythm, figures danced.
These thoughts were immaculate, entranced
bodies with crystal eyes, ivory bone.

So even if they stopped, stood still,
before the band, inside their universe
they danced a choreography in verse.
They gave us movement only spirit can feel.

The Art of Benny Carter

AL YOUNG

There are afternoons in jazz
when a leaf turns and falls
with so much barely noticed purity
that the not so secret meaning of
everything men and women have
tried to do beyond keeping afloat
becomes as clear as ocean air.

13.

OH, MY SOUL IS IN THE WHIRLWIND!

Nocturne at Bethesda

ARNA BONTEMPS

I thought I saw an angel flying low,
I thought I saw the flicker of a wing
Above the mulberry trees; but not again.
Bethesda sleeps. This ancient pool that healed
A host of bearded Jews does not awake.

This pool that once the angels troubled does not move
No angel stirs it now, no Saviour comes
With healing in His hands to raise the sick
And bid the lame man leap upon the ground.

The golden days are gone. Why do we wait
So long upon the marble steps, blood
Falling from our open wounds? and why
Do our black faces search the empty sky?
Is there something we have forgotten? some precious thing
We have lost, wandering in strange lands?

There was a day, I remember now,
I beat my breast and cried, "Wash me God,
Wash me with a wave of wind upon
The barley; O quiet One, draw near, draw near!
Walk upon the hills with lovely feet
And in the waterfall stand and speak.

"Dip white hands in the lily pool and mourn
Upon the harps still hanging in the trees
Near Babylon along the river's edge,
But oh, remember me, I pray, before
The summer goes and rose leaves lose their red."

The old terror takes my heart, the fear
Of quiet waters and of faint twilights.
There will be better days when I am gone
And healing pools where I cannot be healed.
Fragrant stars will gleam forever and ever
Above the place where I lie desolate.

Yet I hope, still I long to live.
And if there can be returning after death
I shall come back. But it will not be here;
If you want me you must search for me
Beneath the palms of Africa. Or if
I am not there then you may call to me
Across the shining dunes, perhaps I shall
Be following a desert caravan.

I may pass through centuries of death
With quiet eyes, but I'll remember still
A jungle tree with burning scarlet birds.
There is something I have forgotten, some precious thing.
I shall be seeking ornaments of ivory,
I shall be dying for a jungle fruit.

You do not hear, Bethesda.
O still green water in a stagnant pool!
Love abandoned you and me alike.
There was a day you held a rich full moon
Upon your heart and listened to the words
Of men now dead and saw the angels fly.
There is a simple story on your face;
Years have wrinkled you. I know, Bethesda!
You are sad. It is the same with me.

good friday

LUCILLE CLIFTON

i rise up above my self
like a fish flying

men will be gods
if they want it

Simon the Cyrenian Speaks

COUNTEE CULLEN

He never spoke a word to me,
And yet He called my name;
He never gave a sign to me,
And yet I knew and came.

At first I said, "I will not bear
His cross upon my back;
He only seeks to place it there
Because my skin is black."

But He was dying for a dream,
And He was very meek,
And in His eyes there shone a gleam
Men journey far to seek.

It was Himself my pity bought;
I did for Christ alone
What all of Rome could not have wrought
With bruise of lash or stone.

Madam and the Minister

Langston Hughes

Reverend Butler came by
My house last week.
He said, Have you got
A little time to speak?

He said, I am interested
In your soul.
Has it been saved,
Or is your heart stone-cold?

I said, Reverend,
I'll have you know
I was baptized
Long ago.

He said, What have you
Done since then?
I said, None of your
Business, friend.

He said, Sister
Have you back-slid?
I said, It felt good—
If I did!

He said, Sister,
Come time to die,
The Lord will surely
Ask you why!
I'm gonna pray
For you!
Goodbye!

I felt kinder sorry
I talked that way
After Rev. Butler
Went away—
So I ain't in no mood
For sin today.

Song of the Whirlwind

FENTON JOHNSON

1

Oh, my God is in the whirlwind,
    I am walking in the valley;
Lift me up, O Shining Father,
To the glory of the heavens,
I have seen a thousand troubles
On the journey men call living,
I have drunk a thousand goblets
From misfortune's bitter winepress,
But to Thee I cling forever,
God of Jacob, God of Rachel.

2

Oh, my soul is in the whirlwind,
    I am dying in the valley,
Oh, my soul is in the whirlwind
And my bones are in the valley;
At her spinning wheel is Mary
Spinning raiment of the lilies,
On her knees is Martha honey
Shining bright the golden pavement,
All the ninety nine is waiting
For my coming, for my coming.

The Creation

JAMES WELDON JOHNSON

And God stepped out on space,
And he looked around and said:
I'm lonely—
I'll make me a world.

And far as the eye of God could see
Darkness covered everything,
Blacker than a hundred midnights
Down in a cypress swamp.

Then God smiled,
And the light broke,
And the darkness rolled up on one side,
And the light stood shining on the other,
And God said: That's good!

Then God reached out and took the light in his hands,
And God rolled the light around in his hands
Until he made the sun;
And he set that sun a-blazing in the heavens.
And the light that was left from making the sun
God gathered it up in a shining ball
And flung it against the darkness,
Spangling the night with the moon and stars.
Then down between
The darkness and the light
He hurled the world;
And God said: That's good!

Then God himself stepped down—
And the sun was on his right hand,
And the moon was on his left;
The stars were clustered about his head,

And the earth was under his feet.
And God walked, and where he trod
His footsteps hollowed the valleys out
And bulged the mountains up.

Then he stopped and looked and saw
That the earth was hot and barren.
So God stepped over to the edge of the world
And he spat out the seven seas—
He batted his eyes, and the lightnings flashed—
He clapped his hands, and the thunders rolled—
And the waters above the earth came down,
The cooling waters came down,

Then the green grass sprouted,
And the little red flowers blossomed,
The pine tree pointed his finger to the sky,
And the oak spread out his arms,
The lakes cuddled down in the hollows of the
        ground,
And the rivers ran down to the sea;
And God smiled again,
And the rainbow appeared,
And curled itself around his shoulder.

Then God raised his arm and he waved his hand
Over the sea and over the land,
And he said: Bring forth! Bring forth!
And quicker than God could drop his hand,
Fishes and fowls
And beasts and birds
Swam the rivers and the seas,
Roamed the forests and the woods,
And split the air with their wings.
And God said: That's good!

Then God walked around,
And God looked around
On all that he had made.
He looked at his sun,

And he looked at his moon,
And he looked at his little stars;
He looked on his world
With all its living things,
And God said: I'm lonely still.

Then God sat down—
On the side of a hill where he could think;
By a deep, wide river he sat down;
With his head in his hands,
God thought and thought,
Till he thought: I'll make me a man!

Up from the bed of the river
God scooped the clay;
And by the bank of the river
He kneeled him down;
And there the great God Almighty
Who lit the sun and fixed it in the sky,
Who flung the stars to the most far corner of the night,
Who rounded the earth in the middle of his hand;
This Great God,
Like a mammy bending over her baby,
Kneeled down in the dust
Toiling over a lump of clay
Till he shaped it in his own image;

Then into it he blew the breath of life,
And man became a living soul.
Amen.   Amen.

Calvary Way

MAY MILLER

How did you feel, Mary,
Womb heavy with Christ Child,
Tasting the dust of uncertain journey?
Were you afraid?
When, winding the swaddling clothes,
You laid Him in the manger,
Were you afraid?
Could you trace nail holes
Under His curling fingers,
Thorn pricks on the forehead?
Could you trace them?

I should bear a warm brown baby,
A new dark world of wonder;
But I fear the nails that pierce the spirit,
The unseen crosses.
How did you feel, Mary,
On the road beyond the star-lit manger,
Up the hill to crucifixion?
Were you afraid?

Holy Days

LARRY NEAL

HOLY THE DAYS OF THE OLD PRUNE FACE JUNKIE MEN.
HOLY THE SCAG FILLED ARMS.
HOLY THE HARLEM FACES
LOOKING FOR SPACE IN THE DEAD ROCK VALLEYS OF THE CITY

HOLY THE FLOWERS
SING HOLY FOR THE RAPED HOLIDAYS
AND BESSIES GUTS SPILLING ON THE MISSISSIPPI
ROAD
SING HOLY FOR ALL OF THE FACES THAT INCHED
TOWARD FREEDOM, FOLLOWED THE NORTH STAR LIKE
HARRIET AND DOUGLASS.
SING HOLY FOR ALL OUR SINGERS AND SINNERS
AND ALL OF THE SHAPES AND STYLES AND FORMS
OF OUR LIBERATION,
HOLY, HOLY, HOLY, FOR THE MIDNIGHT HASSLES
FOR THE GODS OF OUR ANCESTORS BELLOWING
SUNSETS
AND BLUES CHANTING THE TRUTH THAT GAVE US VISION
O GOD MAKE US STRONG AND READY
HOLY, HOLY, HOLY FOR THE DAY WE OPEN OUR EYES, DIG OURSELVES
AND RAISE IN THE SUN OF OUR OWN PEACE AND PLACE AND
SPACE; YES LORD.

mama's God

Carolyn Rodgers

mama's God never was no white man.
her My Jesus, Sweet Jesus never was neither.
the color they had was the color of
her aches and trials, the tribulations of her heart
mama never had no savior that would turn
his back on her because she was black
when mama prayed, she knew who she
was praying to and who she was praying to
didn't and ain't got
no color.

A New Nephilim

AFAA M. WEAVER

After the Lord
laid the world out,
kissed it full with water,
angels made the first life,
coming on the young women
at night singing, rushing
breezes stirring across naked
skin. Giant men were born who
knew all that God knew, becoming
gods themselves, the populated
myths of Greece and Rome. It was
too much. God killed them all
in surging oceans. Their memories—
Ovid's dreams. Now in a
single hundred years, the rape
of night breezes has seeded
the planet with industry,
the thunder the giants made
when they leaped for stars.
God's anger is around us,
seething, swollen with hot breath—
yellow eyes on our disobedience
like bloody fires in the night,
or the eyes of the cats.

Myself When I Am Real

for Charles Mingus

AL YOUNG

The sun is shining in my backdoor
right now.
             I picture myself thru jewels
the outer brittleness gone as I
fold within always.   Melting.

Love of life is love of God
sustaining all life,
                  sustaining me
when wrong or un-self-righteous
in drunkenness & in peace.

                    He who loves me
is me. I shall return to Him always,
my heart is rain, my brain earth,
but there is only one sun & forever
it shines forth one endless poem
of which my ranting, my whole life
is but breath.

            I long to fade back
into this door of sun forever

Revival

KEVIN YOUNG

came early with
June, each tent a hot
angel of healing, the Spirit
catching in women's throats
and anointing the lazy eye
of an uncle. You wanted
nothing more than for that
preacherman from way
out west to lay golden
hands upon you, making
your pain that thing
he spoke of

until you became
a testimony circling
the tent on your own. Lord
how you prayed that week
your knees turning into
the hard-backed pews of early
service, each with a brassy
name in its side; how you
went back each

and every night
filling the aisles with
bodies better left
behind. Back then sin
was a coin rubbed
faceless in the pocket
an offering given
gladly, that clear silver
sound everyone
listened for.

Gray Day in January in La Jolla

for Porter Sylvanus Troupe

QUINCY TROUPE

the day absent of sun, troubles in over plush hilltops
threatening rain, cool hours mist toward noon
wearing gray shawls of vapor, patches of blue peek through
ragged holes punched in clouds, look like anxious eyes of
    scandinavians
worrying through their skins when they see snowstorms coming,
in a place cold & white as anything imaginable, eye look

past green foliage touched with hints of autumn shivering
like a homeless white man in a harlem doorway in february,
look past white ice storms freezing the nation, all the way to the
    capitol,
on martin luther king day, standing there on heated stone, bill
clinton takes his second oath of office, as rumors swirl around him
posing as vultures devouring an abandoned blood kill,

he lays out a vision for the future as good old boys dumped
like pillsbury dough into their rumpled suits fight back yawns, eyes
boring into the back of clinton's head like cold barrels of shotguns,
the cheers of the massive crowd punctuated by gun salutes,
tries beating back the cold of this day sweeping in from the arctic,
flags popping trembling wings crack over the capitol,

as jessye norman takes us where we have to go, singing:
    america, america, God shed his grace on thee, & crown thy good
with brotherhood, from sea to shining sea
but we remember the reality of ennis cosby's senseless death, on this
    day
out here in the west, where everything seems so cozy & warm, where
time wears the laid-back attitude of a surfer crouched on a board,

riding an incoming wave, eye see climbing up invisible ladder rungs,
deep in his imagination, the growing power of my son
porter's angular body, all arms & legs now, eyes peering out innocent
but knowing, laid-back but cold, his mind calculating the distance
his thirteen-year-old body must conquer before he understands
the meaning of roads he has just walked over pigeon-toed,

clouds breaking across tops of hillsides, light shimmying in golden
blue, the sky widening into this moment bright as anywhere
clear & warm, the voice of jessye norman touching the blues breaks
        through
radio, her voice evoking history washes through this poem,
implants hints of lady day's warning of "strange fruit,"
as the threat of another storm gathers itself—as love

& hatred everywhere—north of here, above san francisco,
porter & eye see shadows of clouds lengthening here in la jolla,
see them spreading down hillsides like dark amoebas, mirth,
ragged as edges of daylight slipping toward darkness,
the air cool with mist now, the hour decked out in gray shawls,
cloud vapors now puffing up into shapes of dolphins, whales,

sharks cruising a sky cold as these waters off the coastline

14.

Dear Lovely Death

The Scuba Diver Recovers the Body of a Drowned Child

Gerald Barrax

Maria, she said. No city river
Should take a name like that.
You should have been an island child and dived or fallen
Into water that liquified sunlight. Once,
        in the Bahamas, Maria, I saw
a school of fish frightened by the shadow of a plane.

There aren't enough Marias
Even in the Caribbean with all its light
To give one of you to this waste and muck.
Did you die in the taste of mills and factories? And
        when the shadow passed
over the clear water I was swimming among them.

How much of your life was there to see
To make you almost forget to breathe?
It was here, waiting for you. Scenes
Passing out of all our lives into yours. Bright
        sun. The painted fish
swimming in and out of the coral around me.

Your mother said. God. here under the river.
You were a beautiful girl she said.
All our lives have passed. Your black world blacker
Here where the sun never reaches. Next

summer the sands will be whiter   I will go down deeper
without my mask   and come up and let the air suck my lungs out

when we go up   Maria
she will arrange your hair
and the wind will dry it
sun warms you
she said you were beautiful
she will know

The House of Falling Leaves

WILLIAM STANLEY BRAITHWAITE

The House of Falling Leaves we entered in—
He and I—we entered in and found it fair;
At midnight some one called him up the stair,
And closed him in the Room I could not win.
Now must I go alone out in the din
Of hurrying days: for forth he cannot fare;
I must go on with Time, and leave him there
In Autumn's house where dreams will soon grow thin.

When Time shall close the door unto the house
And open that of Winter's soon to be,
And dreams go moving through the ruined boughs—
He who went in comes out a Memory.
From his deep sleep no sound may e'er arouse,—
The moaning rain, nor wind-embattled sea.

The Rites for Cousin Vit

Gwendolyn Brooks

Carried her unprotesting out the door.
Kicked back the casket-stand. But it can't hold her,
That stuff and satin aiming to enfold her,
The lid's contrition nor the bolts before.
Oh oh. Too much. Too much. Even now, surmise,
She rises in the sunshine. There she goes,
Back to the bars she knew and the repose
In love-rooms and the things in people's eyes.
Too vital and too squeaking. Must emerge.
Even now she does the snake-hips with a hiss,
Slops the bad wine across her shantung, talks
Of pregnancy, guitars and bridgework, walks
In parks or alleys, comes haply on the verge
Of happiness, haply hysterics. Is.

In Honor of David Anderson Brooks, My Father

July 30, 1883—November 21, 1959

GWENDOLYN BROOKS

A dryness is upon the house
My father loved and tended.
Beyond his firm and sculptured door
His light and lease have ended.

He walks the valleys, now—replies
To sun and wind forever.
No more the cramping chamber's chill,
No more the hindering fever.

Now out upon the wide clean air
My father's soul revives,
All innocent of self-interest
And the fear that strikes and strives.

He who was Goodness, Gentleness,
And Dignity is free,
Translates to public Love
Old private charity.

the death of thelma sayles

2/13/59

age 44

LUCILLE CLIFTON

i leave no tracks so my live loves
can't follow. at the river
most turn back, their souls shivering,
but my little girl stands alone on the bank
and watches. i pull my heart out of my pocket
and throw it. i smile as she catches all
she'll ever catch and heads for home
and her children. mothering
has made it strong, i whisper in her ear
along the leaves.

The Charm

RITA DOVE

They called us
the tater bug twins.
We could take a tune
and chew it up, fling
it to the moon
for the crows to eat.

At night he saw him,
naked and swollen
under the backyard tree.
No reason, he replied
when asked why he'd done
it. Thomas woke up
minutes later, thinking
What I need is a drink.

Sunday mornings
fried fish and hominy steaming
from the plates like an oracle.
The canary sang more furious
than ever, but he heard
the whisper: *I ain't dead.*
I just gave you my life.

A Death Song

PAUL LAURENCE DUNBAR

Lay me down beneaf de willers in de grass,
Whah de branch'll go a-singin' as it pass.
   An' w'en I's a-layin' low,
   I kin hyeah it as it go
Singin', "Sleep, my honey, tek yo' res' at las'."

Lay me nigh to whah hit meks a little pool,
An' de watah stan's so quiet lak an' cool,
   Whah de little birds in spring,
   Ust to come an' drink an' sing,
An' de chillen waded on dey way to school.

Let me settle w'en my shouldahs draps dey load
Nigh enough to hyeah de noises in de road;
   Fu' I t'ink de las' long res'
   Gwine to soothe my sperrit bes'
If I's layin' 'mong de t'ings I's allus knowed.

Wedding

RUTH FORMAN

A funeral is a wedding with God
betrothed to him
we are at death finally married
his from before the very beginning of beginnings

death a time of white flowers
veils lifted
and love from the whole spirit

i will tell my children
yes wear black on the outside
tribute the scars of this world
but wear light on the inside
for glory of the one who passed

this is the day of celebration
the day of love and arms to wrap you whole
for the rest of your lives

and i will tell you mother that i am proud to help you gather your
    gown
your thread your stitches shoes and stockings
i am proud to be your waiting girl for that day
i apologize if i ever made you feel rushed or uncomfortable
i will remember the preparation and need
i will remember the pre-wedding days
i will remember them past my own
and i will tell my children
i will tell them

We Assume: On the Death of Our Son, Reuben Masai Harper

Michael S. Harper

We assume
that in 28 hours,
lived in a collapsible isolette,
you learned to accept pure oxygen
as the natural sky;
the scant shallow breaths
that filled those hours
cannot, did not make you fly—
but dreams were there
like crooked palmprints on
the twin-thick windows of the nursery—
in the glands of your mother.

We assume
the sterile hands
drank chemicals in and out
from lungs opaque with mucus,
pumped your stomach,
eeked the bicarbonate in
crooked, green-winged veins,
out in a plastic mask;

A woman who'd lost her first son
consoled us with an angel gone ahead
to pray for our family—
gone into that sky
seeking oxygen,
gone into autopsy,
a fine brown powdered sugar,
a disposable cremation:

We assume
you did not know we loved you.

Nightmare Begins Responsibility

MICHAEL S. HARPER

I place these numbed wrists to the pane
watching white uniforms whisk over
him in the tube-kept
prison
fear what they will do in experiment
watch my gloved stickshifting gasolined hands
breathe *boxcar-information-please* infirmary tubes
distrusting white-pink mending paperthin
silkened end hairs, distrusting tubes
shrunk in his *trunk-skincapped*
shaven head, in thighs
distrusting-white-hands-picking-baboon-light
on this son who will not make his second night
of this wardstrewn intensive airpocket
where his father's asthmatic
hymns of *night-train*, train done gone
his mother can only know that he has flown
up into essential calm unseen corridor
going boxscarred home, *mamaborn, sweetsonchild*
gonedowntown into *researchtestingwarehousebatteryacid*
mama-son-done-gone/me telling her 'nother
train tonight, no music, no breathstroked
heartbeat in my infinite distrust of them:

and of my distrusting self
white-doctor-who-breathed-for-him-all-night
say it for two sons gone,
say nightmare, say it loud
panebreaking heartmadness;
nightmare begins responsibility.

Song for a Suicide

Langston Hughes

Oh, the sea is deep
And a knife is sharp
And a poison acid burns;
But they all bring rest
In a deep, long sleep
For which the tired soul yearns—
They all bring rest in a nothingness
From where no road returns.

Wake

LANGSTON HUGHES

Tell all my mourners
To mourn in red—
Cause there ain't no sense
In my bein' dead.

I hate to die this way with the quiet
Over everything like a shroud.
I'd rather die where the band's a-playin'
Noisy and loud.

Rather die the way I lived—
Drunk and rowdy and gay!
God! Why did you ever curse me
Makin' me die this way?

Suicide's Note

LANGSTON HUGHES

The calm,
Cool face of the river
Asked me for a kiss.

Aunt Jane Allen

FENTON JOHNSON

State Street is lonely today. Aunt Jane Allen has driven her chariot to
    Heaven.
I remember how she hobbled along, a little woman, parched of skin, brown
    as the leather of a satchel and with eyes that had scanned eighty years
    of life.
Have those who bore her dust to the last resting place buried with her the
    basket of aprons she went up and down State Street trying to sell?
Have those who bore her dust to the last resting place buried with her the
    gentle word *Son* that she gave to each of the seed of Ethiopia?

Go Down Death (A Funeral Sermon)

JAMES WELDON JOHNSON

Weep not, weep not,
She is not dead;
She's resting in the bosom of Jesus.
Heart-broken husband—weep no more;
Grief-stricken son—weep no more;
She's only just gone home.

Day before yesterday morning,
God was looking down from his great, high heaven,
Looking down on all his children,
And his eye fell on Sister Caroline,
Tossing on her bed of pain.
And God's big heart was touched with pity,
With the everlasting pity.

And God sat back on his throne,
And he commanded that tall, bright angel standing at his right hand:
Call me Death!
And that tall, bright angel cried in a voice
That broke like a clap of thunder:
Call Death!—Call Death!
And the echo sounded down the streets of heaven
Till it reached away back to that shadowy place,
Where Death waits with his pale, white horses.

And Death heard the summons,
And he leaped on his fastest horse,
Pale as a sheet in the moonlight.
Up the golden street Death galloped,
And the hoof of his horse struck fire from the gold,
But they didn't make no sound.
Up Death rode to the Great White Throne,
And waited for God's command.

And God said: Go down, Death, go down,
Go down to Savannah, Georgia,
Down in Yamacraw,
And find Sister Caroline.
She's borne the burden and heat of the day,
She's labored long in my vineyard,
And she's tired—
She's weary—
Go down, Death, and bring her to me.

And Death didn't say a word,
But he loosed the reins on his pale, white horse,
And he clamped the spurs to his bloodless sides,
And out and down he rode,
Through heaven's pearly gates,
Past suns and moons and stars;
On Death rode,
And the foam from his horse was like a comet in the sky;
On Death rode,
Leaving the lightning's flash behind;
Straight on down he came.

While we were watching round her bed,
She turned her eyes and looked away,
She saw what we couldn't see;
She saw Old Death. She saw Old Death.
Coming like a falling star.
But Death didn't frighten Sister Caroline;
He looked to her like a welcome friend.
And she whispered to us: I'm going home,
And she smiled and closed her eyes.

And Death took her up like a baby,
And she lay in his icy arms,
But she didn't feel no chill.
And Death began to ride again—
Up beyond the evening star,
Out beyond the morning star,
Into the glittering light of glory,
On to the Great White Throne.

And there he laid Sister Caroline
On the loving breast of Jesus.

And Jesus took his own hand and wiped away her tears,
And he smoothed the furrows from her face,
And the angels sang a little song,
And Jesus rocked her in his arms,
And kept a-saying: Take your rest,
Take your rest, take your rest.
Weep not—weep not,
She is not dead;
She's resting in the bosom of Jesus.

Awe

BOB KAUFMAN

At confident moments, thinking on Death
I tell my soul I am ready and wait
While my mind knows I quake and tremble
At the beautiful Mystery of it.

A Poem of Attrition

ETHERIDGE KNIGHT

I do not know if the color of the day
Was blue, pink, green, or August red.
I only know it was summer, a Thursday,
And the trestle above our heads
Sliced the sun into black and gold bars
That fell across our shiny backs
And shimmered like flat snakes on the water,
Worried by the swans, shrieks, jackknives,
And timid gainers—made bolder
As the day grew older.
Then Pooky Dee, naked chieftain, poised,
Feet gripping the black ribs of wood,
Knees bent, butt out, long arms
Looping the air, challenged
The great "two 'n' a half" gainer . . .
I have forgotten the sound of his capped
Skull as it struck the block . . .
The plop of a book dropped? The tear of a sheer blouse?
I do not know if the color of the day
Was blue, pink, green, or August red.
I only know the blood slithered, and
Our silence rolled like oil
Across the wide green water.

Another Poem for Me

(after recovering from an O.D.)

Etheridge Knight

what now
what now dumb nigger damn near dead
what now
now that you won't dance
behind the pale white doors of death
what now   is   to be
to be what you wanna be
or what white / america wants you to be
a lame crawling from nickel bag to nickel bag
be black brother / man be black
and blooming in the night
be black like your fat brother
sweating and straining to hold you
as you struggle against the straps
be black   be black like
your woman   her painted face floating
above you   her hands sliding
                    under the sheets
to take yours   be black like
your mamma sitting in a quiet corner
praying to a white / jesus to save her black boy

what now dumb nigger damn near dead
where is the correctness
the proper posture
the serious love of living
now that death has fled these quiet corridors

Please

Yusef Komunyakaa

Forgive me, soldier.
  Forgive my right hand
         for pointing you
         to the flawless
tree line now
  outlined in my brain.
         There was so much
bloodsky over our heads at daybreak
         in Pleiku, but I won't say
         those infernal guns
         blinded me on that hill.

Mistakes piled up men like clouds
  pushed to the dark side.
    Sometimes I try to retrace
        them, running
          my fingers down the map
            telling less than a woman's body—
we followed the grid coordinates
  in some battalion commander's mind.
        If I could make my mouth
         unsay those orders,
        I'd holler: Don't
          move a muscle.
           Stay put,
& keep your fucking head
down, soldier.

Ambush.
Gutsmoke.
  Last night
    while making love
         I cried out,

Hit the dirt!
I've tried to swallow my tongue.
You were a greenhorn, so fearless,
even foolish, & when I said go, Henry,
you went dancing on a red string
of bullets from that tree line
as it moved from a low cloud.

My Mother

CLAUDE MCKAY

The dawn departs, the morning is begun,
The Trades come whispering from off the seas,
The fields of corn are golden in the sun,
The dark-brown tassels fluttering in the breeze;
The bell is sounding and children pass,
Frog-leaping, skipping, shouting, laughing shrill,
Down the red road, over the pasture-grass,
Up to the schoolhouse crumbling on the hill.
The older folk are at their peaceful toil,
Some pulling up the weeds, some plucking corn,
And others breaking up the sun-baked soil.
Float, faintly scented breeze, at early morn
Over the earth where mortals sow and reap—
Beneath its breast my mother lies asleep.

Going Under

CARL PHILLIPS

So what, if the nurses on this particular shift
are all eunuchs, their slippers, as they
pad the buckled tiles, thin

from dreaming back the cool marble of a history
they remember hearing tales of somewhere,
just history now? So what?

For you, the doctor has shaved his dark, difficult
face, something other than the shit- and
fly-covered walls for your

eyes to travel. For you, his lips close, just
behind and above your head, around snatches
of the St. Matthew Passion—

how many angels, even those in countries less
babbling than this one, can do that?
Captain, be easy, this is only

what it is at last to be falling: why else don't
the doctor's hands, as any stranger's
before, take you anywhere special

now? How else can you not want to touch it, his
dwindling brow, want the darkness coming
down to be his ears, like wings,

unfolding to shade you all the long way home?

Annie Pearl Smith Discovers Moonlight

PATRICIA SMITH

My mother, the sage of Aliceville, Alabama,
didn't believe that men had landed on the moon.
"They can do anything with cameras,"
she hissed to anyone and everyone who'd listen,
even as moonrock crackled
beneath Neil Armstrong's puffed boot.
While the gritty film spun and rewound and we
heard the snarled static of "One small step,"
my mother pouted and sniffed
and slammed skillets into the sink.
She was not impressed.
After all, it was 1969, a year fat with deceit
So many miracles
had proven mere staging for lesser dramas.

But why this elaborate prank
staged in a desert "somewhere out west,"
where she insisted the cosmic gag unfolded?
"They are trying to fool us."
No one argued, since she seemed near tears,
remembering the nervy deceptions of her own skin—
mirrors that swallowed too much,
men who blessed her with touch only as warning.
A woman reduced to juices, sensation and ritual,
my mother saw the stars only as signals for sleep.
She had already been promised the moon.

And heaven too. Somewhere above her head
she imagined bubble-cheeked cherubs
lining the one and only road to salvation,
angels with porcelain faces and celestial choirs
wailing gospel brown enough to warp the seams of paradise.
But for heaven to be real, it could not be kissed,

explored,
strolled upon
or crumbled in the hands of living men.
It could not be the 10 o'clock news,
the story above the fold.

My mother had twisted her tired body into prayerful knots,
worked twenty years in a candy factory,
dipping wrinkled hands into vats of lumpy chocolate,
and counted out dollars with her thin, doubled vision,
so that a heavenly seat would be plumped for her coming.
Now the moon,
the promised land's brightest bauble,
crunched plainer than sidewalk beneath ordinary feet.
And her Lord just lettin' it happen.

"Ain't nobody mentioned God in all this," she muttered
over a hurried dinner of steamed collards and cornbread.
"That's how I know they ain't up there.
Them stars, them planets ain't ours to mess with.
The Lord woulda showed Hisself if them men
done punched a hole in my heaven."
Daddy kicked my foot beneath the table;
we nodded, we chewed, we swallowed.
Inside me, thrill unraveled;
I imagined my foot touching down on the jagged rock,
blessings moving like white light through my veins.

Annie Pearl Smith rose from sleep that night
and tilted her face full toward a violated paradise.
My father told me how she whispered in tongues,
how she ached for a sign
she wouldn't have to die to believe.

Now I watch her clicking like a clock toward deliverance,
and I tell her that heaven still glows wide and righteous
with a place waiting just for her,
fashioned long ago by that lumbering dance
of feet both human and holy.

The Old People Speak of Death

for Grandmother Leona Smith

QUINCY TROUPE

the old people speak of death
frequently, now
my grandmother speaks of those now
gone to spirit, now
less than bone

they speak of shadows that graced
their days, made lovelier by their wings of light
speak of years & of the corpses of years, of darkness
& of relationships buried
deeper even than residue of bone
gone now, beyond hardness
gone now, beyond form

they smile now from ingrown roots
of beginnings, those who have left us
& climbed back through holes the old folks left
inside their turnstile eyes
for them to pass through
eye walk back now, with this poem
through turnstile holes the old folks—ancestors—left inside
their tunneling eyes for me to pass through, walk back to where
eye see them there
the ones who have gone beyond hardness
the ones who have gone beyond form
see them there
darker than where roots began
& lighter than where they go
carrying spirits heavier than stone—
their memories sometimes brighter
than the flash of sudden lightning

& green branches & flowers will grow
from these roots, wearing faces
darker than time & blacker than even the ashes of nations
sweet music will sprout from these flowers & wave petals
like hands caressing love-stroked language
under sun-tongued mornings—
shadow the light spirit in all our eyes

they have gone now, back to shadow
as eye climb back out of the holes of these old peoples'
eyes, those spirits who sing now through this poem
who have gone now back with their spirits
to fuse with greenness
enter stones & glue their invisible traces
as faces nailed upon the transmigration of earth
their exhausted breath now singing guitar blues
voices blowing winds through white ribcages
of these boned days
gone now back to where
years run, darker than where
roots begin, greener than what
they bring—spring
the old people speak of death
frequently, now
my grandmother speaks of those now
gone to spirit, now
less than bone

Solace

MARGARET WALKER

Now must I grieve and fret my little way
into death's darkness, ending all my day
in bitterness and pain, in striving and in stress;
go on unendingly again
to mock the sun with death
and mask all light with fear?
Oh no, I will not cease to lift my eyes
beyond those resurrecting hills;
a Fighter still, I will not cease to strive
and see beyond this thorny path a light.
I will not darken all my days
with bitterness and fear,
but lift my heart with faith and hope
and dream, as always, of a brighter place.

Wake

KEVIN YOUNG

Jesus tucked with cousins into mirrors
this bedroom reflects more saviour
than self, sees relatives whose names
fade with sun until what's left we call
resemblance, kin   *Sign me up*

for the Christian Jubilee

Da Da quilted in a few feet
beneath crosses & ads for sheriff
the hanging judges he nailed
up himself I lie pillows away
restless, sharing beds like years

of Luckies passed between brown
fingers   Soon he is more cough
than words & sleep is the prayer
carrying him through the night   *Write*
my name on the roll

Not so far ago whites wouldn't
touch blackfolks even dead
specially dead
Mr Bones was the richest
most-sought-after negro in town

I spend the whole of night
counting families, lambs, guessing
at unknown masters who left
this legacy of skin angled red
O I've been changed

345

since the Lord has lifted me

Dawn, I start sudden as falling
awake during Sunday sermon, half-
expecting to hear Reverend
talking bad bout us Saturday
night sinners, half-looking round

for an amen corner glare

but finding only Da Da's lips closed
brown & quiet as hymnals in the pew
before me, his breath the paper comfort
of church fans: funeral home on one side
smiling family, a father the other

15.

I DREAM A WORLD

Family Affairs

MAYA ANGELOU

You let down, from arched
Windows,
Over hand-cut stones of your
Cathedrals, seas of golden hair.

While I, pulled by dusty braids,
Left furrows in the
Sands of African beaches.

Princes and commoners
Climbed over waves to reach
Your vaulted boudoirs,

As the sun, capriciously,
Struck silver fire from waiting
Chains, where I was bound.

My screams never reached
The rare tower where you
Lay, birthing masters for
My sons, and for my
Daughters, a swarm of
Unclean badgers, to consume
Their history.

Tired now of pedestal existence
For fear of flying
And vertigo, you descend
And step lightly over
My centuries of horror
And take my hand,

Smiling call me
      Sister.

Sister, accept
That I must wait a
While. Allow an age
Of dust to fill
Ruts left on my
Beach in Africa.

Rhinemaiden

D. L. Crockett-Smith

Who are you, fair-haired lady,
Dissecting me with blue stares?
Why do you watch me only?

Here on the streets of Cologne,
Across the seats and peopled aisles
Of the Strassenbahn, alone

On evenings in the Altstadt,
Near the twilight Cathedral,
You probe and etch my dark heart.

Though Tristan clasps your prim form
As you navigate the crowd,
I rivet you. Am I charmed?

Is it my caramel flesh,
Or the black gloss of coiled hair,
The gnome's goatee—or anguish

In the eyes? Perhaps you see
James Meredith sprawl—shotgunned—
Or hear Dizzy Gillespie

When you watch me. Can I know
What I am beside the moon:
The darkness or a shadow?

I sing your beauty, lady.
For I can never touch one
Foreign as the moon to me.

Open Letter

OWEN DODSON

Brothers, let us discover our hearts again,
Permitting the regular strong beat of humanity there
To propel the likelihood of other terror to an exit.

For at last it is nearly ended: the daily anguish needles
Probing in our brains when alarms crust the air
And planes stab over us.

(Tears screamed from our eyes,
Animals moaned for death, gardens were disguised,
Stumps strained to be whole again.)

For at last it is nearly ended, grass
Will be normal, hillsides
Pleased with boys roaming their bellies.

All the mourning children
Will understand the long word, hallelujah,
Each use for joy will light for them.

The torn souls and broken bodies will be restored,
Primers circulate for everlasting peace,
The doors to hope swung open.

Brothers, let us enter that portal for good
When peace surrounds us like a credible universe.
Bury that agony, bury this hate, take our black hands in yours.

Paradiso

CORNELIUS EADY

In Italy, a scholar is giving an after-dinner talk on her study of Dante and the many questions left unanswered about the afterlife.

For example, where does the shade of the body, the one true and indestructible rainbow vessel, go to wait for the end of time if the head goes one way at the moment of death, and the limbs another?

And I thought of my father, fired to dust in a plain urn, and all the answers I'd learned in church, how all the lost must rise, commuters home at last, from wherever fate has ditched them, with their dishonored ropes and blown equipment, up from the sea, the peat, the misjudged step, the angry fuselage, the air bright from ashes, as will and memory knit.

Will my father's glorified body be the one I'd grown up with, a stocky man, perhaps dressed in his one good suit?

Will he be the young boy I'll never know, Sonny Eady, who wanders off for months at a time, always returning with no accounting of his movements?

Will he be the groom my mother saw, or the shape of the man she claims visited her weeks after his funeral, appearing just to help my mother close this file on their lives, just to tell her *fare-thee-well, woman, I'll never see you no more?*

How can this be done? is one question the scholar is here to work on, and as she places our hands into Dante's; and night gathers in the mountains, I think that every hymn is a flare of longing, that the key to any heaven is language.

Walking Down Park

NIKKI GIOVANNI

walking down park
amsterdam
or columbus do you ever stop
to think what it looked like
before it was an avenue
did you ever stop to think
what you walked
before you rode
subways to the stock
exchange (we can't be on
the stock exchange
we are the stock
exchanged)

did you ever maybe wonder
what grass was like before
they rolled it
into a ball and called
it central park
where syphilitic dogs
and their two-legged tubercular
masters fertilize
the corners and side-walks
ever want to know what would happen
if your life could be fertilized
by a love thought
from a loved one
who loves you

ever look south
on a clear day and not see
time's squares but see
tall Birch trees with sycamores

touching hands
and see gazelles running playfully
after the lions
ever hear the antelope bark
from the third floor apartment

ever, did you ever, sit down
and wonder about what freedom's freedom
would bring
it's so easy to be free
you start by loving yourself
then those who look like you
all else will come
naturally

ever wonder why
so much asphalt was laid
in so little space
probably so we would forget
the Iroquois, Algonquin
and Mohicans who could caress
the earth

ever think what Harlem would be
like if our herbs and roots and elephant ears
grew sending
a cacophony of sound to us
the parrot parroting black is beautiful black is beautiful
owls sending out whooooo's making love . . .
and me and you just sitting in the sun trying
to find a way to get a banana from one of the monkeys
koala bears in the trees laughing at our listlessness

ever think it's possible
for us to be
happy

Dream Variation

Langston Hughes

To fling my arms wide
In some place of the sun,
To whirl and to dance
Till the white day is done.

Then rest at cool evening
Beneath a tall tree
While night comes on gently,
   Dark like me—
That is my dream!

To fling my arms wide
In the face of the sun,
Dance! whirl! whirl!
Till the quick day is done.
Rest at pale evening. . . .
A tall, slim tree. . . .
Night coming tenderly
   Black like me.

I Dream a World

Langston Hughes

I dream a world where man
No other man will scorn,
Where love will bless the earth
And peace its paths adorn.
I dream a world where all
Will know sweet freedom's way,
Where greed no longer saps the soul
Nor avarice blights our day.
A world I dream where black or white,
Whatever race you be,
Will share the bounties of the earth
And every man is free,
Where wretchedness will hang its head
And joy, like a pearl,
Attends the needs of all mankind—
Of such I dream, my world!

For Russell and Rowena Jelliffe

LANGSTON HUGHES

And so the seed
Becomes a flower
And in its hour
Reproduces dreams
And flowers.

And so the root
Becomes a trunk
And then a tree
And seeds of trees
And springtime sap
And summer shade
And autumn leaves
And shape of poems
And dreams—
And more than tree.

And so it is
With those who make
Of life a flower,
A tree, a dream
Reproducing (on into
Its own and mine
And your infinity)
Its beauty and its life
In you and me.

And so it was
And is with you:
The seed, the flower,
The root, the tree,
The dream, the you.

This poem I make

(From poems you made)

For you.

Lift Ev'ry Voice and Sing

JAMES WELDON JOHNSON

Lift ev'ry voice and sing,
Till earth and heaven ring,
Ring with the harmonies of Liberty;
Let our rejoicing rise
High as the list'ning skies,
Let it resound loud as the rolling sea.
Sing a song full of the faith that the dark past has taught us,
Sing a song full of the hope that the present has brought us;
Facing the rising sun of our new day begun,
Let us march on till victory is won.

Stony the road we trod,
Bitter the chast'ning rod.
Felt in the days when hope unborn had died;
Yet with a steady beat,
Have not our weary feet
Come to the place for which our fathers sighed?
We have come over a way that with tears has been watered,
We have come, treading our path through the blood of the
        slaughtered,
Out from the gloomy past,
Till now we stand at last
Where the white gleam of our bright star is cast.

God of our weary years,
God of our silent tears,
Thou who hast brought us thus far on the way;
Thou who hast by Thy might,
Led us into the light,
Keep us forever in the path, we pray.
Lest our feet stray from the places, our God, where we met Thee,
Lest our hearts, drunk with the wine of the world, we forget Thee;
Shadowed beneath Thy hand,
May we forever stand,
True to our God,
True to our native land.

The Gods Wrote

KEORAPETSE KGOSITSILE

We are breath of drop of rain,
Grain of seasand in the wind
We are root of baobab,
Flesh of this soil,
Blood of Congo brush, elegant
As breast of dark cloud
Or milk flowing through the groaning years

We also know
Centuries with the taste
Of white shit down to the spine . . .

The choice is ours,
So is the life,
The music of our laughter reborn
Tyityimba or boogaloo, passion of
The sun-eyed gods of our blood
Laughs in the nighttime, in the daytime too
And across America, vicious cities
Clatter to the ground. Was it not

All written by the gods!
Turn the things! I said let
Them things roll to the rhythm of our movement
Don't you know this is a love supreme!
John Coltrane, John Coltrane, tell the ancestors
We listened, we heard your message
Tell them you gave us tracks to move,

Trane, and now we know
The choice is ours
So is the mind and the matches too
The choice is ours

So is the beginning
"We were not made eternally to weep"
The choice is ours
So is the need and the want too
The choice is ours
So is the vision of the day

I Have a Dream

Pat Parker

i have a dream
   no—
   not Martin's
though my feet moved
   down many paths.
it's a simple dream—

i have a dream
   not the dream of the vanguard
   not to turn this world—
     all over
not the dream of the masses—
   not the dream of women
   not to turn this world
    all
       over
it's a simple dream—

In my dream—
   i can walk the streets
    holding hands with my lover

In my dream—
   i can go to a hamburger stand
    & not be taunted by bikers on a holiday.

In my dream—
   i can go to a public bathroom,
    & not be shrieked at by ladies—

In my dream—
   i can walk ghetto streets
    & not be beaten up by my brothers.

In my dream—
    i can walk out of a bar
       & not be arrested by the pigs

I've placed this body
    placed this mind
    in lots of dreams—
    in Martin's & Malcolm's—
    in Huey's & Mao's—
    in George's & Angela's—
    in the north & south
       of Vietnam & America
          & Africa

i've placed this body & mind
    in dreams—
    dreams of people—

    now i'm tired—
    now you listen!
       i have a dream too.
       it's a simple dream.

Daybreak

STERLING PLUMPP

every day
i find a new life.
my love for freedom,
our right
to wear robes
as we please,
never sets.
black voices
dance in my soul
like anxious sparkles.
every black man
is an epic,
sung
in the soft keys
of survival.
o i want,
i want,
i want
to hear
be near
all my brothers
when i die

Now

MARGARET WALKER

Time to wipe away the slime
from inner rooms of thinking,
and covert skin of suffering;
indignities and dirt
and helpless degradation;
from furtive relegation
to the back doors and dark alleys
and the balconies of waiting
in the cleaning rooms and closets
with the washrooms and the filthy
privies marked "For Colored Only"
and the drinking-soda fountains
tasting dismal and disgusting
with a dry and dusty flavor
of deep humiliation;
hearing vulgars shout to mothers
"Hey you, nigger girl, and girlie!
Auntie, Ant, and Granny;
My old mammy was a wonder
and I love those dear old darkies
who were good and servile nigras
with their kerchiefed heads and faces
in their sweet and menial places."
Feeling hats and blood comingled
in a savage supplication
full of rites and ceremonies
for the separate unequal—
re-enforced by mobs who mass
with a priest cult and klan
robed and masked in purest White
marking Kleaged with a Klux
and a fiery burning cross.
Time to wipe away the slime.
Time to end this bloody crime.

In C. W.'s Closet

Afaa Michael Weaver

I climb the C scale on the old piano.
On the third finger, I forget
the crossover step like a man forgets
a kiss. You chuckle, rupture
the stillness of Indian Pond, hustle
over to the window, look out over
the blueberry field you knew as a child.
Then you turn gracefully as someone
sixty years younger with the gray hair
blonde, the brittle frame full
with flesh. You turn and beckon me
to your closet, to the past.

In the personal closet your father stands
in photographs where you toddle along,
you and Elizabeth at the end
of the Gilded Age. She has her gumption,
you your willingness to obey
the root of the law over our tainted bodies,
the blossom of the law over our souls.
Your father stands in his rebuke
of DuBois, the black rabble rouser,
after the Niagara Falls convention.
Disparate fingers were called together,
before I settled into your domain,
a heavy bird with inchoate wings.

You pull back and sigh, eye me
with the deadlock desperation we sing
when we know the flower must wither,
the stone must crumble, the friend must go.
We unlock from our fixed gaze
on your father in his belief

in segregation. We move together
into the kitchen, young and old,
black and white, poor and rich.
Our bodies are so close they pattern a rhythm
above the evening news with Tom Brokaw,
above the world as it wanes, moans.
Our breath mingles with the night.

The Song Turning Back Into Itself 2

A song for little children

AL YOUNG

Always it's either
a beginning
or some end:
the baby's being born
or its parents are
dying, fading on
like the rose
of the poem
withers, its light going out
while gardens come in
to bloom

Let us stand on streetcorners
in the desolate era
& propose a new kind
 of crazyness

Let us salute one another
one by one
two by two
the soft belly
moving toward
the long sideburns
the adams apple
or no apple at all

Let there be
in this crazyness
a moon
a violin
a drum

Let the beautiful brown girl
join hands with
her black sister
her golden sister
her milkskinned sister
their eternal wombs
turning with the moon

Let there be a flute
to squeal above
the beat & the bowing
to open us up
that the greens
the blues
the yellows
the reds
the silvers &
indescribable rusts
might flow out
amazingly
& blend
with the wind

Let the wobbly spin
of the earth
be a delight
wherein
a caress forms
the most perfect circle

Let the always be love
the beginning be love
love the only
possible
end

BIOGRAPHIES

ALEXANDER, ELIZABETH [1962–]

Born in Harlem, New York, Alexander received her B.A. from Yale, her M.A. from Boston University and her Ph.D. in English from the University of Pennsylvania. She has taught at Haverford, Smith, the University of Chicago, and the University of Pennsylvania. She currently teaches at Yale. Her awards include a Pushcart Prize and a National Endowment for the Arts Fellowship. Her books include *The Venus Hottentot*; *Body of Life*; and *Antebellum Dream Book*.

ALLEN, SAMUEL [1917–]

Born in Columbus, Ohio, Allen received his B.A. from Fisk and his J.D. from Harvard Law School. After a career in law and government service in the United States and Europe, Allen began a second career as a professor, teaching at Tuskegee, Wesleyan, and Boston University. His books of poetry include *Ivory Tusks and Other Poems*; *Paul Vesey's Ledger*; and *Every Round and Other Poems*.

ANGELOU, MAYA [1928–]

Angelou was born Marguerite Johnson in St. Louis, Missouri. In 1969 she published *I Know Why The Caged Bird Sings*, widely regarded as an autobiographical classic. In 1981 she became a chaired professor at Wake Forest University in North Carolina. In 1993 she read her commemorative poem "On the Pulse of the Morning" at President Clinton's inauguration. Her books include *Gather Together in My Name*; *All God's Children Need Traveling Shoes*; and *The Complete Collected Poems of Maya Angelou*.

AUBERT, ALVIN [1930–]

Born in Lutcher, Louisiana, Aubert received his B.A. from Southern University in Louisiana, and his M.A. from the University of Michigan. He taught at Southern University, Illiniois, Oregon, Wayne State University, and the State University of New York at Fredonia. In 1975, he founded *Obsidian*, a journal of black scholarly and creative writing. His books include *Against the Blues*; *South Louisiana: New and Selected Poems*; *If Winter Come: Collected Poems, 1967–1992*; and *Harlem Wrestler and Other Poems*.

Baraka, Amiri [1934–]

Baraka was born Everett Leroi Jones in Newark, New Jersey. He earned his B.A. in English from Howard University. Celebrated as a leader of the Black Arts Movement, Baraka is an influential poet, dramatist, and cultural critic. For many years, he was professor of Drama and of Africana Studies at the State University of New York, Stony Brook. His critical works include *Blues People* and *Black Art*. His books of poetry include *Preface to a Twenty-Volume Suicide Note* and *Transbluesency: The Selected Poetry of Amiri Baraka/Leroi Jones (1961–1995)*. His plays include *Dutchman* and *The Slave*.

Barlow, George [1948–]

Born in Berkeley, California, Barlow earned a B.A. from California State University at Hayward and an M.A. and M.F.A. from the University of Iowa. He is currently a professor at Grinnell College in Iowa, where he has chaired the American Studies department. He has published two volumes of poetry, *Gabriel* and *Gumbo*.

Barrax, Gerald [1933–]

Born in Alabama, Barrax received a B.A. from Duquesne University and an M.A. from the University of Pittsburgh. He has served as a poetry editor for the journals *Obsidian* and *Callaloo* and is a professor of English at North Carolina State University. His books of poetry include *Another Kind of Rain*; *The Deaths of Animals and Lesser Gods*; *Leaning Against the Sun*; and *From a Person Sitting in Darkness: New and Selected Poems*.

Bontemps, Arna [1902–1973]

Born in Alexandria, Louisiana, Bontemps earned a B.A. from Pacific Union College, and a M.L.S. from the University of Chicago. A prolific writer, he published poetry and prose, children's books, plays, and anthologies of African American literature. He served as the head librarian at Fisk University from 1943 to 1966, and then as a professor of literature at the University of Illinois, Chicago, and at Yale. His awards included fellowships from the Rosenwald and Guggenheim Foundations. With Langston Hughes he co-edited *The Book of Negro Folklore* and *The Poetry of the Negro*. His novels include *God Sends Sunday* and *Black Thunder*. His only volume of verse is *Personals*.

BRAITHWAITE, WILLIAM STANLEY [1878–1962]

Born in Boston, Massachusetts, Braithwaite taught at Atlanta University and was editor of the highly regarded annual *Anthology of Magazine Verse and Yearbook of American Poetry* and literary editor of the *Boston Evening Transcript*. In 1918, He received the Springarn Medal, the NAACP's highest honor. His books of verse include *Lyrics of Life and Love; The House of Falling Leaves;* and *Selected Poems.*

BRIDGES, CONSTANCE QUATERMAN

Bridges' awards include a New Jersey Arts Council Fellowship. Her work has been featured in numerous magazines, including *African American Review.* She recently completed *Lions Don't Eat Us,* a collection of poems based on her mother's journal.

BROOKS, GWENDOLYN [1917–2000]

Born in Topeka, Kansas, Brooks was educated in Chicago at public high schools and Wilson Junior College. She won two Guggenheim fellowships in the 1940s and was awarded the Pulitzer Prize for poetry in 1950 for her collection, *Annie Allen.* In 1968 she was named the Poet Laureate of Illinois. Author of the novel *Maud Martha,* she also published books of verse, including *A Street in Bronzeville; The Bean Eaters; Selected Poems; In the Mecca; Family Pictures;* and *Riot.*

BROWN, STERLING [1901–1989]

Born in Washington, D.C., Brown was educated at Dunbar High School and received his B.A. from Williams and his M.A. from Harvard. He taught at Virginia Seminary for three years, and then at Howard University until 1969. An outstanding critic as well as a poet, he was co-editor of the landmark anthology *The Negro Caravan,* with Arthur P. Davis and Ulysses Lee. He published three books of poetry: *Southern Road; The Last Ride of Wild Bill and Eleven Narrative Poems;* and *The Collected Poems of Sterling Brown;* as well as a collection of essays, *A Son's Return.*

CLIFTON, LUCILLE [1936–]

Born in Depew, New York, Clifton attended Howard University and Fredonia State Teachers College (now the State University of New York at Fredonia). Her awards include fellowships from the National Endowment for the Arts, a Lannan Literary Award, and an Emmy. She has been Poet Laureate of the state of Maryland, a Chancellor of the Academy of American Poets, and currently teaches at St. Mary's College in Maryland. She won the National Book Award for *Blessing the Boats: New and Selected Poems 1998–2000*. Her other books include *Good Times; An Ordinary Woman; The Terrible Stories*; and *Generations: A Memoir*.

COLEMAN, ANITA SCOTT [1890–1960]

Born in Mexico, Coleman graduated from the New Mexico Teachers College before moving to Los Angeles. Her fiction and poetry appeared in numerous magazines, including the *Crisis; Opportunity*; and the *Messenger*. She was also the author of two volumes of verse: *Reason for Singing* and *The Singing Bells*.

COLEMAN, WANDA [1946–]

Born in Los Angeles, Coleman has received fellowships from the National Endowment for the Arts and the Guggenheim Foundation. In 1999 she was awarded the Lenore Marshall Poetry Prize for *Bathwater Wine*. Her other books of poetry include *A War of Eyes and Other Stories; Hand Dance*; and *Mercurochrome: New Poems*. She has also written *Mambo Hips and Make Believe: A Novel*.

CORNISH, SAM [1935–]

Born in Baltimore, Maryland, Cornish studied at Goddard College in Vermont and at Northwestern University. He has taught at Coppin State College. He has edited literary journals and anthologies and written numerous children's books. His awards include a grant from the National Endowment for the Arts. His books include *Generations and Other Poems; Sam's World; Songs of Jubilee: New and Selected Poems*; and *1935: A Memoir*.

CORTEZ, JAYNE [1936–]

Born in Fort Huachuca, Arizona, Cortez co-founded the Watts Repertory Theatre in Los Angeles in 1964. She has been a teacher and writer-in-residence at Rutgers University and she founded Bola Press in 1972. She has won fellowships from the National Endowment for the Arts and the New York Foundation for the Arts as well as the American Book Award. Her books of poetry include *Pissstained Stairs and the Monkey Man's Wares; Mouth on Paper; Coagulations: New and Selected Poems*; and *Somewhere in Advance of Nowhere*.

COTTER JR., JOSEPH SEAMON [1895–1919]

Cotter was born in Louisville, Kentucky. He studied for two years at Fisk University before illness forced him to return home, where he became an editor and writer for the Louisville *Leader*. He produced three books of poetry: *The Band of Gideon and Other Lyrics*; *Out of the Shadows*; and *Poems*.

CROCKETT-SMITH, D.L. [1954–]

Born in Tuskegee, Alabama, Smith received his B.A. from New College of Florida and his Ph.D. from the University of Chicago. He currently teaches at Williams College. He has won fellowships from the National Endowment for the Humanities and the American Council of Learned Studies. With Cornel West and Jack Salzman, he co-edited *The Encyclopedia of African American Culture and History*. His books of verse include *Cowboy Amok* and *Civil Rites*.

CROUCH, STANLEY [1945–]

Born in Los Angeles, California, Crouch attended East Los Angeles Junior College and Southwest Junior College. He co-founded the Jazz at Lincoln Center program, where he is an artistic consultant. He has taught at Columbia University. He has won the Whiting Writer's Prize as well as the John D. and Catherine T. MacArthur Foundation Fellowship. He has written for numerous publications, including the *Village Voice* and the *New York Daily News*. His essay collections include *Notes of a Hanging Judge*; *The All-American Skin Game; or, The Decoy of Race: The Long and Short of It, 1990–1994*; and *Always in Pursuit: Fresh American Perspectives, 1995–1997*. He is also the author of a novel, *Don't the Moon Look Lonesome*, and a collection of poetry entitled *Ain't No Ambulances for No Nigguhs Tonight*.

CULLEN, COUNTEE [1903–1946]

Born Countee Porter in Louisville, Kentucky, Cullen attended De Witt Clinton High School before receiving his B.A. from New York University and his M.A. from Harvard. He taught at Frederick Douglass Junior High School in New York. A novelist, as well as one of the foremost poets of the Harlem Renaissance, his awards include the Springarn Medal of the NAACP, the Harmon Foundation Literary Award, and a Guggenheim Fellowship. His books include *Color*; *The Black Christ and Other Poems*; *One Way to Heaven*; *On These I Stand: An Anthology of the Best Poems of Countee Cullen*; and *My Soul's High Song: The Collected Writings of Countee Cullen, Voice of the Harlem Renaissance*.

DERRICOTTE, TOI [1941–]

Born in Detroit, Michigan, Derricotte earned her B.A. from Wayne State University and her M.A. from New York University. She currently teaches at the University of Pittsburgh. She has won awards from the Folger Shakespeare Library, the National Endowment for the Arts and the Poetry Society of America, as well as a Pushcart Prize. She is co-founder of Cave Canem, a workshop retreat for African American poets. Her books include *The Empress of the Death House*; *Natural Birth*; *Captivity*; *Tender*; and a literary memoir, *The Black Notebooks*.

DIXON, MELVIN [1950–1992]

Born in Stamford, Connecticut, Dixon received his B.A. from Wesleyan and his M.A. and Ph.D. from Brown. He taught at Williams College and Queens College, New York. He won a National Endowment for the Arts Poetry Fellowship and a Fulbright lectureship in Senegal. An accomplished poet, author, translator, and critic, his books include the novels *Trouble the Water* and *Vanishing Rooms*; the poetry collections *Change of Territory* and *Love's Instruments*; and a volume of criticism, *Ride Out the Wilderness*.

DODSON, OWEN [1914–1983]

Born in Brooklyn, New York, Dodson received his B.A. from Bates College, and his B.F.A. from Yale. He taught at Atlanta University and Howard University. He won Rosenwald and Guggenheim Fellowships and a short story award from the *Paris Review*. A prolific author, he wrote more than thirty plays and operas. His books of poetry include *Powerful Long Ladder*; *The Confession Stone*; and *The Harlem Book of the Dead*.

DOVE, RITA [1952–]

Born in Akron, Ohio, Dove received her B.A. from Miami University in Ohio and her M.F.A. from the University of Iowa. She has taught at Arizona State University, Tuskegee, and the University of Virginia. In 1993 she became the first African American to be named poet laureate of the United States. She also won the Pulitzer Prize in 1997 for *Thomas and Beulah*. Her other books include *The Yellow House on the Corner*; *Grace Notes*; and *Selected Poems*.

DU BOIS, W. E. B. [1868–1963]

Du Bois was born in Great Barrington, Massachusetts. A graduate of Fisk University and Harvard, Du Bois also studied at the University of Berlin. A professor at Atlanta University, he left to help found the National Association for the Advancement of Colored People (NAACP) in 1910, the same year he founded the *Crisis*, which became the most widely read African American magazine of its era. His many books include *The Suppression of the African Slave-Trade to the United States; The Philadelphia Negro; and The Souls of Black Folk.*

DUMAS, HENRY [1934–1968]

Born in Sweet Home, Arkansas, Dumas attended City College in New York before joining the U.S. Air Force. After a four-year tour of duty, he studied at Rutgers University. He taught at Hiram College in Ohio and was director of language workshops at Southern Illinois University. His books of poetry include *Play Ebony, Play Ivory; Goodbye, Sweetwater; and Knees of a Natural Man: The Selected Poetry of Henry Dumas.*

DUNBAR, PAUL LAURENCE [1872–1906]

Born in Dayton, Ohio, Dunbar attended Dayton High School, where he was president of his class as well as the only African American student. Working as an elevator operator in Dayton, in 1893 he published his first volume of poetry, *Oak and Ivy.* In 1898 he was appointed to a clerkship in the U.S. Library of Congress. Acclaimed for both his dialect verse and traditional poetry, he also wrote four novels. His books include *Majors and Minors; Lyrics of Lowly Life;* and the novel *The Sport of the Gods.*

DUREM, RAY [1915–1963]

Born in Seattle, Durem served in the U.S. Navy from the age of fourteen. He fought in the Spanish Civil War and later lived in Mexico for many years. His work has appeared in such publications as *Negro Digest* (later *Black World*) and *Umbra,* as well as the anthologies *New Negro Poets: USA;* and *I Am the Darker Brother.* His collection *Take No Prisoners* was published in 1972.

EADY, CORNELIUS. [1954–]

Born in Rochester, New York, Eady attended Monroe Community College and Empire State College there. He is the author of several volumes of verse, including *Victims of the Latest Dance Craze, You Don't Miss Your Water,* and *Brutal Imagination.* Eady has won many awards from organizations such as the Academy of American Poets, the John Simon Guggenheim Foundation, and the National Endowment for the Arts. In 1995 he joined the faculty at the University of Notre Dame in South Bend, Indiana.

EMANUEL, JAMES A. [1921–]

Born in Alliance, Nebraska, Emanuel received his B.A. from Howard, his M.A. from Northwestern and his Ph.D. from Columbia. He taught for many years at City College of New York before emigrating to France. He won the John Hay Whitney Award and a Saxton Memorial Fellowship. His works include *Black Man Abroad: The Toulouse Poems*; *The Broken Bowl*; and *Whole Grain: Collected Poems, 1959–1989*.

EVANS, MARI [1923–]

Born in Toledo, Ohio, Evans attended the University of Toledo. She has taught literature and creative writing at Indiana University, Northwestern, Spelman College, Purdue, the State University of New York at Albany, Washington University, and Cornell. She has won the John Hays Whitney Fellowship, as well as fellowships from Yaddo and the National Endowment for the Arts. Her books of poetry include *I Am a Black Woman*; *Nightstar: 1973–1978*; *A Dark and Splendid Mass*; and *How We Speak*.

FORBES, CALVIN [1945–]

Born in Newark, New Jersey, Forbes studied at the New School for Social Research at Rutgers University and received his M.F.A. from Brown. He has taught at Emerson College, Tufts University, Howard University, and the School of the Art Institute of Chicago. He has held fellowships from the Illinois Arts Council, the National Endowment for the Arts, and Bread Loaf. His books include *Blue Monday*; *From the Book of Shine*; and *The Shine Poems*.

FORMAN, RUTH [1968–]

Born in Falmouth, Massachusetts, Forman earned a B.A. from the University of California, Berkeley, and an M.A. from the USC School of Cinema and Television. She won the Barnard New Women Poets Prize in 1993 for her collection *We Are the Young Magicians*. Her other awards include the Durfee Artist Fellowship and the Pen Oakland Josephine Miles Award for Poetry. Her second book of poetry is entitled *Renaissance*.

GILBERT, CHRISTOPHER [1948–]

Born in Birmingham, Alabama, Gilbert studied at the University of Michigan. He won the Walt Whitman Prize in 1983 for his book *Across the Mutual Landscape*. He teaches at the College of New Jersey.

GIOVANNI, NIKKI [1943–]

Born in Knoxville, Tennessee, Yolanda Cornelia "Nikki" Giovanni, Jr. received her B.A. from Fisk and her M.A. from the University of Pennsylvania. An important figure in the Black Arts Movement, she won the Langston Hughes Award for Distinguished Contributions to Arts and Letters in 1996. She is a professor of English and Black Studies at Virginia Tech University. Her books include *Black Feeling, Black Talk*; *Ego Tripping and Other Poems for Young People*; *My House: Poems*; and *The Collected Poetry of Nikki Giovanni: 1968–1998*.

GISCOMBE, C.S. [1950–]

Born in Dayton, Ohio, Giscombe has taught at Syracuse, Brown, Illinois State University, Pennsylvania State University and Cornell. He was won fellowships from the National Endowment for the Arts, the Illinois Arts Council, and the Fulbright Foundation. He won the Carl Sandburg Prize for his collection of poems *Giscome Road*. His other books include *Here*; and *Into and Out of Dislocation*.

GRIMKÉ, ANGELINA WELD [1880–1958]

Born in Boston, Massachusetts, Weld graduated from the Boston Normal School of Gymnastics in 1902 then moved to Washington, D.C., where she taught English at the Armstrong Manual Training School until 1916 and then at Dunbar High until 1930. Her poetry was published in magazines and anthologies including *Crisis*, *Opportunity*, *The New Negro* and *Caroling Dusk*. Her works include the play *Rachel*.

HARPER, FRANCES E.W. [1825–1911]

Harper was born in Baltimore, Maryland. Orphaned by the age of three, she left school early to work in domestic service. In the early 1850s she taught at schools in Ohio and Pennsylvania. She then joined the antislavery movement and lectured extensively throughout the United States. Her books include *Poems on Miscellaneous Subjects*; *Sketches of Southern Life*; and the novel *Iola Leroy*.

HARPER, MICHAEL S. [1938–]

Brooklyn-born, Harper earned his B.A. and M.A. from California State University, and his M.F.A. from the University of Iowa. Since 1970 he has taught

English at Brown. Between 1988 and 1993, he served as the first Poet Laureate of Rhode Island. His other honors include a Guggenheim Fellowship and awards from the National Endowment for the Arts and the Poetry Society of America. His books include *Dear John, Dear Coltrane; History Is Your Own Heartbeat; Healing Song for the Inner Ear;* and *Songlines in Michaeltree: New and Collected Poems.*

HAYDEN, ROBERT [1913–1982]

Robert Hayden was born Asa Bundy Sheffey in Detroit, Michigan. He earned his B.A. from Detroit City College (now Wayne State University) and his M.A. from the University of Michigan. For several years he was a professor of English at Fisk University. His awards include the grand prize for poetry at the First World Festival of Negro Arts and an appointment as consultant in poetry to the Library of Congress. His books include *Heart-Shape in the Dust: Poems; Ballad of Remembrance; Angle of Ascent: New and Selected Poems;* and *Collected Poems.*

HEMPHILL, ESSEX [1957–1995]

Born in Chicago, Hemphill studied at the University of Maryland and the University of the District of Columbia. In 1993 he was artist in residence at the Getty Museum in Los Angeles. His other honors include the National Library Association's Gay and Lesbian Book Award, a Lambda Literary Award, and the Gregory Kolovakos Award for AIDS Writing. His books include *Earth Life; Conditions;* and *Ceremonies: Prose and Poetry.*

HERNTON, CALVIN C. [1934–2001]

Born in Chattanooga, Tennessee, Hernton earned a B.A. from Talladega College and an M.A. from Fisk. He co-founded *Umbra* magazine in 1963. He taught at Benedict College, Alabama A&M, Southern University, and Oberlin College. His books include *The Coming of Chronos to the House of Nightsong: An Epical Narrative of the South; Medicine Man;* and *The Red Crab Gang and Black River Poems.*

HOAGLAND, EVERETT [1942–]

Born in Philadelphia, Hoagland earned a B.A. from Lincoln and an M.A. from Brown. A publishing poet since his college days, he has taught at various colleges and universities but mainly at the University of Massachusetts, Dartmouth, from which he retired as an associate professor of English in 2004. He has won the Gwendolyn Brooks Award and two Massachusetts Poetry Fellowships. His books include *Black Velvet; This City and Other Poems;* and *Here: New and Selected Poems.*

HUGHES, LANGSTON [1902–1967]

Born in Joplin, Missouri and reared in Lawrence, Kansas, Hughes studied at Columbia before earning his B.A. at Lincoln University. A leading figure in the Harlem Renaissance, he is considered one of the most influential poets of the 20th century for his groundbreaking use of black music and vernacular speech. In addition to his poetry, he also published fiction, drama, journalism, autobiography, and children's books. His books of poetry include *The Weary Blues; Fine Clothes to the Jew; Montage of a Dream Deferred;* and *The Collected Poems of Langston Hughes.* With Arna Bontemps he edited *The Book of Negro Folklore* and *The Poetry of the Negro.*

JACKSON, MURRAY [1926–2002]

Born in Detroit, Jackson served in the Navy in WWII, and then returned to earn a B.A. and an M.A. from Wayne State University. Jackson was the founding president of Wayne County Community College in Detroit and a longtime member of the Wayne State University Board of Governors. He taught at the University of Michigan and Wayne State University. He also served as the first executive director of the Detroit Council of the Arts. His books include *Watermelon Rinds and Cherry Pits; Woodland Sketches: Scenes from Childhood;* and *Bobweaving Detroit: The Selected Poems of Murray Jackson.*

JEFFERS, LANCE [1919–1985]

Born in Fremont, Nebraska, Jeffers studied at the University of California, Berkeley, before joining the Army to serve in Europe in WWII. He later received a B.A. and M.A. from Columbia. He taught at the University of Denver, the University of Toronto, California State University, Long Beach, and North Carolina State University. His books include *My Blackness is The Beauty of This Land; When I Know the Power of My Black Hand; O Africa, Where I Baked My Bread; Grandsire;* and a novel, *Witherspoon.*

JOHNSON, FENTON [1888–1958]

Born in Chicago, Illinois, Johnson was educated at Northwestern and at the University of Chicago, where he earned his B.A. Johnson later studied journalism at Columbia. A journalist, he edited two magazines, and taught college in Louisville, Kentucky. His books include three poetry collections: *A*

Little Dreaming; Visions of the Dusk; Songs of the Soil; a book of essays, *For the Highest Good;* and a collection of short stories, *Tales of Darkest America.*

JOHNSON, GEORGIA DOUGLAS [1880–1966]

Born in Georgia, Johnson earned her B.A. in Music from the Atlanta University Normal School, and then studied at the Oberlin Conservatory and the Cleveland College of Music. A longtime resident of Washington, D.C., she was appointed to the Department of Labor by President Coolidge in 1925. A prolific writer, she published journalism and drama, as well as poetry. Her books include *The Heart of a Woman; Bronze: A Book of Verse; An Autumn Love Cycle;* and *Share My World.*

JOHNSON, HELENE [1907–1995]

Born in Boston, Massachusetts, Johnson studied at Boston University before moving to New York. Her poetry was published in such magazines as *Opportunity; Vanity Fair;* and *Fire!!.*

JOHNSON, JAMES WELDON [1871–1938]

Born in Jacksonville, Florida, Johnson earned his B.A. from Atlanta University. He was principal of Stanton School in Jacksonville until 1901, when he moved to New York to write music. He served as U.S. consul in Venezuela and Nicaragua, and later was elected the first African American president of the NAACP. He also taught at Fisk University. His books include a novel, *The Autobiography of an Ex-Coloured Man;* and several volumes of poetry, including *Fifty Years and Other Poems; God's Trombones: Seven Negro Sermons in Verse;* and *Saint Peter Relates an Incident.* He also edited the landmark anthology *The Book of American Negro Poetry.*

JORDAN, JUNE [1936–2002]

Born in Harlem, Jordan studied at Barnard College and the University of Chicago. She taught at City College of New York, Sarah Lawrence, and Yale. For many years she was a professor of African American Studies and Women's Studies at the University of California, Berkeley, where she founded the Poetry for the People program. Her awards include a grant from the Rockefeller Foundation, a Prix de Rome, and a fellowship from the National Endowment for the Arts. Her books include *Things That I Do in the Dark; Some Changes; Naming Our Destiny: New and Selected Poems; Kissing God Goodbye;* and *Affirmative Acts: Political Essays.*

KAUFMAN, BOB [1925–1986]

Born in New Orleans, Louisiana, Kaufman left school as a boy and spent the next twenty years in the U.S. Merchant Marine. Later, he studied literature at the New School in New York City. A colleague of Allen Ginsberg, Jack Kerouac, and other Beat poets, Kaufman helped found *Beatitude* magazine in 1959. His books include *Abomunist Manifesto; Solitudes Crowded with Loneliness; Golden Sardine;* and *The Ancient Rain: Poems 1956–1978.*

KGOSITSILE, KEORAPETSE [1938–]

Born in South Africa, Keorapetse has taught at Sarah Lawrence College, the University of Dar es Salaam, the University of Nairobi, and the University of Gaborone. He has won the Gwendolyn Brooks Prize for Poetry, as well as awards from the National Endowment for the Arts, the New York Council on the Arts, and the Rockefeller Foundation. His books include *My Name is Afrika; Places and Bloodstains; The World is Here;* and *When the Clouds Clear.*

KNIGHT, ETHERIDGE [1931–1991]

Born in Corinth, Mississippi, Knight served in the U.S. Army from 1947 to 1951. In 1960 he was convicted of robbery and sentenced to eight years in Indiana State Prison. In 1968 Dudley Randall's Broadside Press published Knight's *Poems from Prison.* Knight taught at the University of Pittsburgh, the University of Hartford, and Lincoln University. He won fellowships from the Guggenheim Foundation, the National Endowment for the Arts, and the Poetry Society of America. His books include *Poems from Prison; A Poem for Brother / man; Belly Song and Other Poems; Born of a Woman: New and Selected Poems;* and *The Essential Etheridge Knight.*

KOMUNYAKAA, YUSEF [1947–]

Born in Bogalusa, Louisiana, Komunyakaa served in the U.S. Army from 1965 until the early 1970s, including service in Vietnam. He received his B.A. from the University of Colorado, his M.A. from Colorado State University, and his M.F.A from the University of California at Irvine. He won the Pulitzer Prize for Poetry in 1994 for *Neon Vernacular: New and Selected Poems 1977–1989.* In 1999 he was elected a Chancellor of the Academy of American Poets. His books include *Copacetic; I Apologize for the Eyes in My Head; Dien Cai Dau; Magic City;* and *Pleasure Dome: New & Collected Poems, 1975–1999.*

LATTANY, KRISTIN [1931–]

Born in Philadelphia, Lattany studied at the University of Pennsylvania, where she later taught for 23 years. A prolific writer of fiction for children and adults, she won the Moonstone Black Writing Celebration Achievement Award in 1996. Her books include *God Bless the Child; The Soul Brother and Sister Lou; The Landlord;* and *Kinfolks.*

LORDE, AUDRE [1934–1992]

Born in Harlem, Lorde received a B.A. from Hunter College and an M.L.S. from Columbia University. She taught at Tougaloo College, Lehman College, John Jay College of Criminal Justice, and Hunter College. Her honors include selection as Poet Laureate of New York and an American Book Award in 1989 for *A Burst of Light*. Her books of poetry include *The First Cities; From a Land Where Other People Live; The Black Unicorn;* and *Undersong: Chosen Poems Old and New.* She also wrote the influential collection *Sister Outsider: Essays and Speeches.*

MACKEY, NATHANIEL [1947–]

Born in Miami, Florida, Mackey received a B.A. from Princeton and a Ph.D. from Stanford. He is a professor of Literature at the University of California at Santa Cruz and has been a Chancellor of the Academy of American Poets. He is editor of *Hambone* magazine. His books include *Four for Trane; Septet for the End of Time; Eroding Witness; School of Udhra;* and *Whatsaid Serif.*

MADGETT, NAOMI LONG [1923–]

Born in Norfolk, Virginia, Madgett earned a B.A. from Virginia State College (now Virginia State University) and an M.Ed. from Wayne State University. She has taught at Eastern Michigan University. In 1993 she won an American Book Award for her editorial work at Lotus Press, a leading publisher of black poetry. In 2001 she was named Poet Laureate of Detroit. Her books of poetry include *Songs to a Phantom Nightingale; One and the Many; Star By Star; Exits and Entrances;* and *Remembrances of Spring: Collected Early Poems.*

MAJOR, CLARENCE [1936–]

Born in Atlanta, Georgia, Major received his B.S. from the State University of New York and his Ph.D. from the Union for Experimenting Colleges and Universities. He has taught at numerous colleges and universities and currently teaches at the University of California, Davis. A poet and novelist, his awards include a Western States Book Award for Fiction, a Pushcart Prize, and a Fulbright Fellowship. His books include *Fires That Burn in Heaven; Inside Diameter: The France Poems; Dirty Bird Blues: A Novel;* and *Configurations: New & Selected Poems 1958–1998.*

McELROY, COLLEEN J. [1935–]

Born in St. Louis, Missouri, McElroy received her B.A. from Kansas City College and her Ph.D. from the University of Washington, where she now teaches. In 1985 she won the American Book Award for her poetry collection *Queen of the Ebony Isles.* Her books of poetry include *Travelling Music* and *What Madness Brought Me Here: New and Selected Poems, 1968–88.* She has also written two collections of fiction, *Jesus and Fat Tuesday* and *Driving Under the Cardboard Pines.*

McKAY, CLAUDE [1889–1948]

Claude McKay was born in Clarendon Parish, Jamaica. He studied briefly at the Tuskegee Institute and at Kansas State College. Recognized as one of the first artists of the Harlem Renaissance, his novel *Home to Harlem* was the first novel by an African American to become a bestseller. His other books include *Constab Ballads; Spring in New Hampshire and Other Poems; Harlem Shadows; The Dialect Poetry of Claude McKay;* and *The Passion of Claude McKay: Selected Poetry and Prose 1912–1948.*

MILLER, E. ETHELBERT [1950–]

Born in New York City, New York, Miller received his B.A. from Howard University, where he was elected director of the African American Resource Center in 1974. He is founder and director of the *Ascension* poetry reading series, a Washington, D.C. forum for young and emergent poets. He has won the Columbia Merit Award and the O.B. Hardison Jr. Poetry Prize. His books include *Andromeda, Season of Hunger/Cry of Rain: Poems 1975–1980; First Light: New and Selected Poems;* and *How We Sleep on the Nights We Don't Make Love.*

MILLER, MAY [1899–1995]

Born in Washington, D.C., Miller received her B.A. from Howard University and later studied at American University and Columbia. She was poet-in-residence at the University of Wisconsin and Exeter Academy. Her books include *Into the Clearing; Dust of Uncertain Journey; Halfway to the Sun;* and *Collected Poems.*

Moss, Thylias [1954–]

Born in Cleveland, Ohio, Moss received a B.A. from Oberlin College and an M.A. from the University of New Hampshire. A professor of English at the University of Michigan, her awards include fellowships from the John D. and Catherine T. MacArthur and Guggenheim Foundations, a Witter Bynner Award for Poetry, and a Whiting Award. Her books include *Hosiery Seams on a Bowlegged Woman; Pyramid of Bone; At Redbones; Small Congregations: New and Selected Poems;* and *Slave Moth: A Narrative in Verse.*

Mullen, Harryette [1953–]

Born in Alabama, Mullen earned a B.A. from the University of Texas and an M.A. and a Ph.D. from the University of California, Santa Cruz. She has won awards from the Texas Institute of Letters and the Helene Wurlitzer Foundation of New Mexico as well as the Gertrude Stein Award in Innovative American Poetry. She has taught at Cornell and now teaches at UCLA. Her books include *Tree Tall Woman; Trimmings; S*PeRM**K*T;* and *Sleeping with the Dictionary.*

Neal, Larry [1937–1981]

Born in Atlanta, Neal received his B.A. from Lincoln University and his M.A. from the University of Pennsylvania. With Amiri Baraka, he co-edited *Black Fire: An Anthology of Afro-American Writing,* which became a central text of the Black Arts Movement. His other works include *Black Boogaloo: Notes on Black Liberation; Hoodoo Hollerin' Bebop Ghosts;* and two plays, *The Glorious Monster in the Bell of the Horn* and *In an Upstate Motel.*

Nicholas, A. X. [1943–]

Nicholas is the editor of *Woke Up This Mornin': Poetry of the Blues* and *The Poetry of Soul.*

Parker, Pat [1944–1989]

Born in Houston, Texas, Parker moved to Oakland, California in the early 1970s. An ardent political activist, she was involved with the Black Panther Party and the Black Women's Revolutionary Council and helped to form the Women's Press Collective. Her books include *Movement in Black; Pit Stop; Womanslaughter;* and *Jonestown and Other Madness.*

Patterson, Raymond [1929–2001]

Born in Harlem, Patterson earned a B.A. from Lincoln University and an M.A. from New York University. He taught at New York City College, where he founded the annual Langston Hughes Festival. His books of poetry include *26 Ways of Looking at a Black Man*; *The Negro and His Needs*; and *Elemental Blues*.

Phillips, Carl [1959–]

Originally from Boston, Phillips received a B.A. from Harvard University and M.A.s from Boston University and the University of Massachusetts, Amherst. He has taught at Harvard, Boston University, and the University of Iowa Writers Workshop. He is a professor at Washington University, St. Louis. He has won the Kingsley Tufts Poetry Award, two Pushcart Prizes, and fellowships from the Guggenheim Foundation, the National Endowment for the Humanities, the Library of Congress, and the Academy of American Poets. His books include *In the Blood*; *Cortege*; *From the Devotions*; *Pastoral*; and *The Rest of Love: Poems*.

Plumpp, Sterling [1940–]

Born in Clinton, Mississippi, Plumpp earned his B.A. and his M.A. from Roosevelt University in Chicago. For many years he taught English and African American Studies at the University of Illinois, Chicago. He has won two Illinois Arts Council Literary Awards and the Carl Sandburg Literary Award for Poetry. His books include *Ornate with Smoke*; *Johannesburg and Other Poems*; *Half Black, Half Blacker*; *Black Rituals*; and *The Mojo Hands Call, I Must Go*.

Redmond, Eugene B. [1937–]

Born in St. Louis, Missouri, Redmond earned a B.A. from Southern Illinois University and an M.A. from Washington University. He has been poet-in-residence and visiting professor at Oberlin College, California State University, Sacramento, and the University of Missouri. He currently teaches at Southern Illinois University, Edwardsville where he edits *Drumvoices Revue*. He has won a Pushcart Prize, a National Endowment for the Arts Fellowship, and an American Book Award. His books include *A Tale of Two Toms, or Tom-Tom (Uncle Toms of East St. Louis & St. Louis)*; *The Eye in the Ceiling: Selected Poems*; *Sentry of the Four Pillars*; and *Drumvoices: The Mission of Afro-American Poetry, A Critical History*.

RIVERS, CONRAD KENT [1933–1968]

Born in Atlantic City, New Jersey, Rivers earned a B.A. from Wilberforce University before pursuing graduate studies at Chicago Teachers' College, Indiana University, and Temple University. His books include *Perchance to Dream; These Black Bodies and This Sunburnt Face; The Still Voice of Harlem;* and *The Wright Poems.*

RODGERS, CAROLYN [1945–]

Born in Chicago, Illinois, Rodgers earned a B.A. from Roosevelt University and an M.A. from the University of Illinois, Chicago. A founding member of the Third World Press, her awards include the Conrad Kent Rivers Memorial Fund Award and the Poet Laureate Award of the Society of Midland Authors. Her books include *Paper Soul; Songs of a Blackbird; how i got ovah: New and Selected Poems;* and *Morning Glory: Poems.*

SANCHEZ, SONIA [1934–]

Born Wilsonia Benita Driver in Birmingham, Alabama, Sanchez received her B.A. from Hunter College. She has taught at San Francisco State University, Amherst College, and Temple University, where she was the named first President's Fellow. She has won an American Book Award, the Pennsylvania Governor's Award for Excellence in the Humanities, a National Endowment for the Arts Award, and a Pew Fellowship in the Arts. Her books include *Homecoming; We a Baddddd People; homegirls & handgrenades; Generations: poetry, 1969–1985;* and *Shake Loose My Skin: New and Selected Poems.*

SMITH, PATRICIA [1955–]

A journalist as well as a poet, Patricia Smith has been a columnist for the *Boston Globe, Ms. Magazine,* and the online magazine *Afazi.* Her awards include the Carl Sandburg Literary Award and four National Slam Poetry Championships. Her books include *Life According to Motown; Big Towns, Big Talk;* and *Close to Death.*

STEPTOE, LAMONT B. [1949–]

Born in Pittsburgh, Pennsylvania, Steptoe earned a B.A. from Temple University and served in the Vietnam War. A poet, photographer, publisher, and activist, Steptoe founded Whirlwind Press. His awards include fellowships from the Pennsylvania Council on the Arts and the Pew Charitable Trust.

His books include *In the Kitchens of the Master; Uncle's South China Sea Blue Nightmare; Crimson River;* and *Mad Minute.*

TOLSON, MELVIN B. [1900–1966]

Born in Moberly, Missouri, Tolson received his B.A. from Lincoln University and his M.A. from Columbia University. He taught at Wiley College and Langston University, and received a chair in the humanities at Tuskegee University. He served as mayor of Langston for four terms in the 1950s. His awards include *Poetry* magazine's Bess Hokin Prize and the title of Poet Laureate of Liberia. His books include *Libretto for the Republic of Liberia; Harlem Gallery: Book I, The Curator;* and *A Gallery of Harlem Portraits.*

TOOMER, JEAN [1894–1967]

Toomer was born in Washington; D.C. He financed his college education by working various jobs, but although he studied at five institutions (including the University of Wisconsin, the American College of Physical Training in Chicago, and the City College of New York) he never received a degree. While serving as superintendent at a school for blacks in Georgia, he was inspired to write the novel *Cane,* considered a masterpiece of the Harlem Renaissance. After the book's publication, Toomer lived in Europe before joining the Quakers in Pennsylvania. His other books include *The Wayward and the Seeking: A Collection of Writings by Jean Toomer;* and *The Collected Poems of Jean Toomer.*

TRETHEWEY, NATASHA [1966–]

Born in Gulfport, Mississippi, Trethewey earned a B.A. from the University of Georgia, an M.A. from Hollins College, and an M.F.A. from the University of Massachusetts. She has won the inaugural Cave Canem Poetry Prize and a Guggenheim Fellowship, as well as a Bunting Fellowship from the Radcliffe Institute for Advanced Study at Harvard. She has taught at Auburn University and currently teaches at Emory University. Her books are *Domestic Work* and *Bellocq's Ophelia.*

TROUPE, QUINCY [1939–]

Born in New York City, Troupe studied at Grambling College (now Grambling State University). He has taught at the University of California at Los Angeles, Ohio University, the University of California at Berkeley, the University of Ghana at Legon, and the City University of New York. He retired as professor emeritus at the University of California, San Diego. His prizes include two American Book Awards and a Peabody Award. His books include *Embryo Poems, 1967–1971; Snake-Back Solos: Selected Poems, 1969–1977; Skulls Along the River; Choruses;* and *Transcircularities: New and Selected Poems.*

WALKER, MARGARET [1915–1998]

Born in Birmingham, Alabama, Walker received her B.A. from Northwestern University and her M.F.A. from the University of Iowa Writers' Workshop. She taught at Jackson State University where she founded the Institute for the Study of the History, Life, and Culture of Black People (now renamed the Margaret Walker Alexander National Research Center). Her poetry collection *For My People* won the Yale Younger Poets' Award. Her other books include *Prophets for a New Day; October Journey; This is My Century: New and Collected Poems,* and the novel *Jubilee.*

WANIEK, MARILYN NELSON [1946–]

Born in Cleveland, Ohio, Waniek received her B.A. from the University of California at Davis, her M.A. from the University of Pennsylvania, and her Ph.D. from the University of Minnesota. She was appointed professor of English at the University of Connecticut at Storrs in 1988. Her books include *For The Body; Mama's Promises; The Homeplace; Magnificat: Poems;* and *The Fields of Praise: New and Selected Poems.*

WEAVER, AFAA M. [1951–]

Afaa M. Weaver, formerly known as Michael S. Weaver, was born in Baltimore, Maryland. He studied at the University of Maryland, College Park before leaving to do factory work. He later earned an M.F.A. from Brown University. A playwright and journalist as well as a poet, Weaver teaches at Simmons College in Boston, and is editor of the journal, *Obsidian II.* His awards include fellowships from the National Endowment for the Arts and the Pew Charitable Trust. His books include *Water Song; Talisman; The Ten Lights of God;* and *Multitudes: Poems Selected and New.*

WILLIAMS, DELORES S. [1939–]

Williams earned a B.A. from the University of Louisville, an M.A. from Columbia University, and a Ph.D. from Union Theological Seminary. She was a professor of theology and culture at Union Theological Seminary in New York City and a contributing editor of *Christianity and Crisis*. She is the author of *Sisters in the Wilderness: The Challenge of Womanist God-Talk*.

WILLIAMS, SHERLEY ANNE [1944–1999]

Born in Bakersfield, California, Williams received her B.A. from Fresno State University and her M.A. from Brown University. She taught at California State University, Fresno, the University of California, San Diego, and the University of Ghana. Her books include *Give Birth to Brightness: A Thematic Study in Neo-Black Literature; The Peacock Poems; Some One Sweet Angel Chile;* and a novel, *Dessa Rose*.

YOUNG, AL [1939–]

Born in Ocean Springs, Mississippi, Young received his B.A. from the University of California, Berkeley. A novelist and memoirist as well as a poet, he has lectured and taught at various colleges and universities, including Stanford, where he was named a Wallace Stegner Fellow. His other honors include the Joseph Henry Jackson Award and fellowships from the Guggenheim Foundation, the National Endowment for the Arts, and the Fulbright Foundation. With Ishmael Reed, he co-founded the journals *Quilt* and *Yardbird*. His books include *Dancing; Collected Poems, 1958–1990; The Sound of Dreams Remembered: Poems 1990–2000;* and the novels *Sitting Pretty* and *Who Is Angelina?*.

YOUNG, KEVIN [1970–]

Born in Lincoln, Nebraska, Young received his B.A. from Harvard University and his M.F.A. from Brown University. He has taught at the University of Georgia and currently teaches at Indiana University. His awards include the Zacharis First Book Award from *Ploughshares* magazine for *Most Way Home*, a Stegner Fellowship in Poetry at Stanford University, and Guggenheim Foundation and MacDowell Colony Fellowships. His other books include *To Repel Ghosts* and *Jelly Roll: A Blues*.

CREDITS

"Father's Day" from *Whispers and Secrets* by E. Ethelbert Miller. Copyright © 1998. Reprinted by permission of Black Classic Press, P.O. Box 13414, Baltimore, Maryland 21203.

"Incantation (for jonetta)" from *Season of Hunger/Cry of Rain* by E. Ethelbert Miller. Copyright © 1982 by E. Ethelbert Miller. Reprinted by permission of E. Ethelbert Miller.

"Jasmine" from *First Light: New and Selected Poems* by E. Ethelbert Miller. Copyright © 1994. Reprinted by permission of E. Ethelbert Miller.

"She Is Flat On Her Back (for K. F.)" from *Season of Hunger/Cry of Rain* by E. Ethelbert Miller. Copyright © 1982 by E. Ethelbert Miller. Reprinted by permission of E. Ethelbert Miller.

"Calvary Way" from *Dust of Uncertain Journey* by May Miller (Lotus Press, 1975). By permission of Lotus Press.

"Gift From Kenya" from *Dust of Uncertain Journey* by May Miller (Lotus Press, 1975). By permission of Lotus Press.

"Accessible Heaven" from *Last Chance by the Tarzan Holler* by Thylias Moss. Copyright © 1998 by Thylias Moss. Reprinted by permission of Persea Books, Inc. (New York).

"Lessons From a Mirror" from *Pyramid of Bone* by Thylias Moss. Reprinted by permission of the University Press of Virginia.

"One For All Newborns" from *Small Congregations: New and Selected Poems* by Thylias Moss. Copyright © 1983, 1990, 1991, 1993 by Thylias Moss. Reprinted by permission of HarperCollins Publishers, Inc.

"Anatomy" from *Blues Baby: Early Poems* by Harryette Mullen. Used by permission of Harryette Mullen and Associated University Presses.

"Blah Blah" from *Sleeping with the Dictionary* by Harryette Mullen. Reprinted by permission of the University of California Press.

"Exploring the Dark Continent" from *Sleeping with the Dictionary* by Harryette Mullen. Reprinted by permission of the University of California Press.

"Eyes in the Back of Her Head" from *Blues Baby: Early Poems* by Harryette Mullen. Used by permission of Harryette Mullen and Associated University Presses.

"Annie Pearl Smith Discovers Moonlight" from *Big Towns, Big Talk* by Patricia Smith. Copyright © 1992 by Patricia Smith. Reprinted by permission of Zoland Books, Cambridge, Massachusetts.

"A Hambone Gospel" by Lamont B. Steptoe. Reprinted by permission of Lamont B. Steptoe.

"For Etheridge Knight" by Lamont B. Steptoe. Reprinted by permission of Lamont B. Steptoe.

"There is a House" by Lamont B. Steptoe. Reprinted by permission of Lamont B. Steptoe.

"Three Legged Chairs" by Lamont B. Steptoe. Reprinted by permission of Lamont B. Steptoe.

"To the Father of Me" by Lamont B. Steptoe. Reprinted by permission of Lamont B. Steptoe.

"Lambda" by Melvin B. Tolson. Reprinted by permission of Melvin B. Tolson.

"Song of the Son" from *Cane* by Jean Toomer. Copyright © 1923 by Boni & Liveright, renewed 1951 by Jean Toomer. Used by permission of Liveright Publishing Corporation.

"Amateur Fighter" from *Domestic Work* by Natasha Trethewey, published by Graywolf Press, 2000. Reprinted by permission of Natasha Trethewey.

"Flounder" from *Domestic Work* by Natasha Trethewey, published by Graywolf Press, 2000. Reprinted by permission of Natasha Trethewey.

"Gray Day in La Jolla" from *Transcircularities* by Quincy Troupe. Copyright © 2001 by Quincy Troupe. Reprinted by permission of Coffee House Press, Minneapolis, Minnesota, USA, www.coffeehousepress.com.

"Old Black Ladies Standing on Bus Stop Corners #2" from *Avalanche* by Quincy Troupe. Copyright © 1996. Reprinted by permission of Coffee House Press.

"Poem for my Father (for Quincy Trouppe, Sr.)" from *Avalanche* by Quincy Troupe. Copyright © 1996. Reprinted by permission of Coffee House Press.

"Reflections on Growing Older" from *Weather Reports: New and Selected Poems* by Quincy Troupe. Copyright © 1991, 2002 by Quincy Troupe. Reprinted by permission of Quincy Troupe.

INDEX